Table of Contents

1. Definitions
2. Acknowledgments
3. Foreword: What is "SMART DREAMS"?
4. Introduction
5. Part 1: SMART builds connection!
6. Introduction to Part One
7. Chapter 1: (S)pecific – "Don't beat around the bush"
8. Chapter 2: (M)otivating – "Don't be dry"
9. Chapter 3: (A)ttentive – "Pay attention"
10. Chapter 4: (R)elevant – "Make it make sense"
11. Chapter 5: (T)iming – "It's not about you"
12. Part 2: DREAMS builds confidence!
13. Introduction to Part Two
14. Chapter 6: (D)river – "Let them drive!"
15. Chapter 7: (R)elationships – "Define a SAFE team!"
16. Chapter 8: (E)ducation – "Elevate their mindset!"

17. Chapter 9: (A)ccountability – "Let them own their choices!"

18. Chapter 10: (M)otivation – "Define a WHY!"

19. Chapter 11: (S)pirituality – "Define a life purpose!"

20. Afterword: SMART DREAMS Coaching

Definitions

SMART DREAMS = A therapeutic empowerment lifestyle designed to transform trauma into self-confidence, clarity of personal identity, and intentional decision-making. (Aka as a transformative movement that empowers individuals to thrive with resilience and confidence in their unique identity and potential.

Dreamer = High risk teen and young adult who have strength and confidence to achieve their DREAMS, but have insecurities that hold them back in anger, anxiety, depression, and lack of trust.

SMART Communication = An engagement tool to help professionals connect with Dreamers who have trauma or one another in a therapeutic and empowering manner. Also, a way to engage with someone when sharing our DREAMS, aspirations, or needs.

DREAMS Mindset = A lifestyle mindset that equips Dreamers with personal habits designed to build confidence and resilience, empowering them to achieve their "DREAMS."

Acknowledgments

This book reflects a few life experiences that have created the life I live today, but it is those I have gotten the chance to learn from and credit for being SMART when connecting with me and empowering my DREAMS, getting me to where I am today to be confident enough to write this book.

God - Life has truly been a journey leading up to this point. From many lows to many highs, but it's you who have anointed my life with your grace and mercy and have gotten me thus far.

Pam (My Foster Mother) - Mom, it is often believed that "we only get one life to live", and while this may be true in physical life, I know it's not in our spiritual life. And that is because of you. When I was at the lowest times in my life as a Dreamer in foster care, you saved me, and when I hit rock bottom again as a young adult, you supported me. Without you, your faith in God, and your commitment to your children, I would not have the spiritual strength to be faithful and resilient as I am.

Matt (My Mentor Turned Father) - "Pops", I don't even know why you're still here, laughing my ass off. I'm just joking. I know exactly why. You're a true guardian angel sent from heaven. From me telling you in your face "hell naw" to being my mentor, to bailing me out of jail on several occasions, and hanging out with me when I used to sag my pants below my butt, SMH at myself, haha, you never judged me. Not only did you not judge me, but you continued to reaffirm your openness to be accepted in my life how I saw fit and that beyond the program, no matter what, our connection could last forever. Today, 14+ years later, you're no longer my mentor, but now my father and the inspiration in life to be a better father, business leader, and all-around man.

Teresa (My Bio Mother) - Mother, while although I know you're still in pain and hurting from your mistakes in the past, I want you to know that you're an amazing woman. I realize that nobody in this world is perfect, we will all make mistakes, but it is not our mistakes that define us. Without your story I wouldn't have had the chance to experience the foster care system and learn 1st hand of the life young people must experience every day when their families abuse or neglect them. Your story is what gave me a foundation to be strong, courageous, and loving while overcoming and trying to change an abusive and challenging system. Your story is a lot, and I hope you share it one day, but what I mean specifically for the world to know, is your heart, your love, and most importantly your love and faith in God. I am Michael Williams and will inspire and motivate the world because your story is my story. Love you!

Dr. Carol Edwards (My Guardian Mentor)

To the woman whose spirit radiates love, wisdom, and grace—

Thank you for being a living example of what it means to move through the world with kindness, patience, and compassion, even in the midst of chaos and turmoil. You are a force—nationally respected, widely admired, and deeply wise—yet you choose to slow down, to be present, and to truly know people beyond their titles or circumstances. That alone is a rare and powerful gift.

But even more, I want to thank you for what you poured into this book—for taking the time to walk beside me, page by page, chapter by chapter, ensuring this wasn't just a book full of inspiration, but one grounded in lived experience, truth, and healing. You made sure that the voice of a young man with passion, pain, and purpose came through—not from ego or insecurity, but from authenticity, growth, and love.

You helped me protect the heart of this work, while shaping it with wisdom that speaks to generations. Your fingerprints are woven into every word, and your support gave me the confidence to share my story not just as a survivor—but as a servant leader.

I am forever grateful for your presence, your guidance, and your belief in me. This book would not be the same without you—and neither would I.

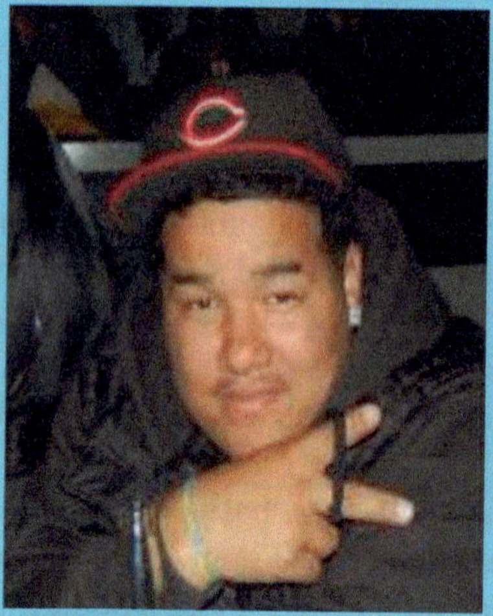

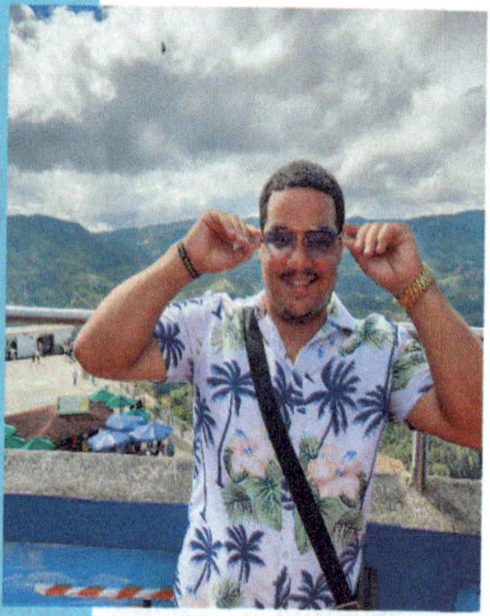

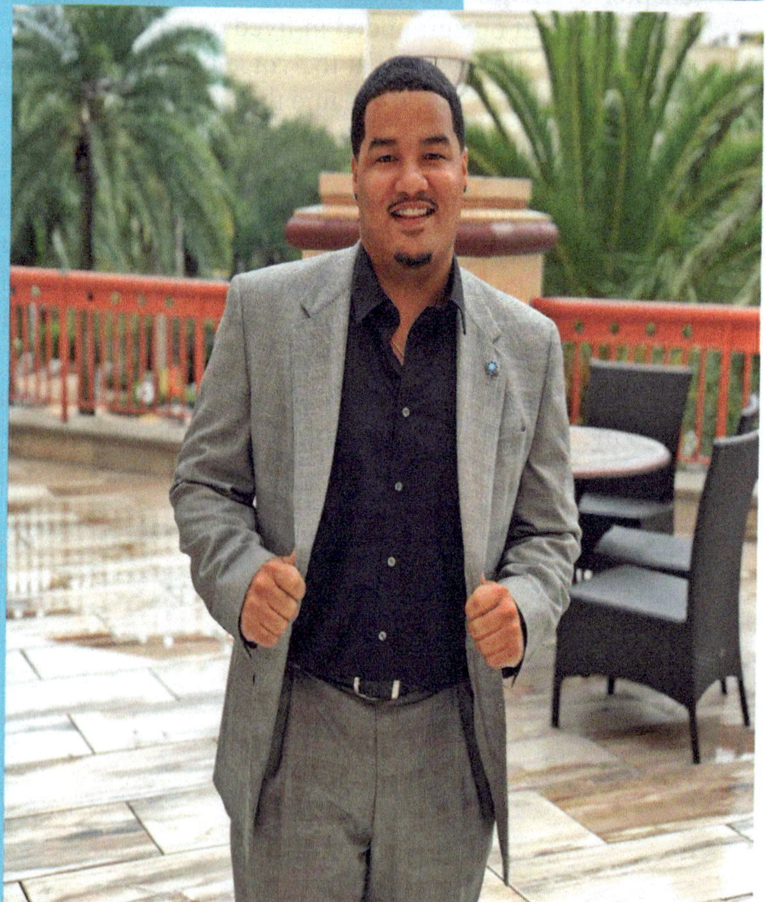

Foreword: What is "SMART DREAMS"?

All young people today have "DREAMS". Social media is filled with lifestyles that heavily influence their daily behaviors, thoughts, and perspectives. Many try to mimic these lifestyles, but when faced with an honest conversation or an opportunity to apply what they mimic, they become afraid, distant, or even create unnecessary drama. Why? I believe because deep down, their trauma holds them back, convincing them to devalue and avoid the very opportunities that could change their lives.

Have you ever seen a young person do this? While this may not be true for everyone, it is a common reality for many Dreamers today, especially those from the foster care system. I know this because I was one of them. Back when I was in the system as a young adult, I constantly sabotaged opportunities, and sometimes, even now, I catch myself slipping into old patterns. The root of this behavior isn't just immaturity or disinterest—it's unhealed trauma. Trauma shapes how young people perceive themselves and the world around them, often leaving them feeling unworthy, unconfident, and disconnected from their potential.

For Dreamers in foster care, the message they often internalize is that they are unwanted or unloved, simply because they are not with their families.

As they navigate the system and day-to-day life, their minds aren't focused on discovering their strengths or envisioning their future. Instead, they are preoccupied with survival—where they will sleep, whether they'll fit into a home where they feel disconnected, or if they'll be bullied without proper protection from their caregiver. This constant state of survival prevents them from developing relationships, forming connections, and establishing the core values and principles needed to thrive socially, emotionally, mentally, physically, and spiritually.

Young people living in this survival mode aren't building confidence; they are living in the shadow of their fears, past failures, and heartaches. In other words, they are stuck in a cycle perpetuated by their trauma—a cycle that holds them back from valuing the opportunities that could change their lives. Helping them break free requires intentional effort, guided support, and a framework like SMART DREAMS.

*

The Impact of Trauma on Decision-Making and Opportunities

Trauma has a profound way of shaping how young people perceive the world around them and, more importantly, themselves. When you grow up in an environment where trust is broken, stability is fleeting, and emotional safety is nonexistent, it's no surprise that opportunities feel more like threats than possibilities. A Dreamer who has experienced trauma often views the world through a lens of skepticism and self-preservation. This mindset leads to behaviors that many interpret as disinterest or defiance, but in reality, it's a defense mechanism.

When a young person feels unworthy or incapable of achieving their dreams, they unconsciously avoid situations that might expose their vulnerabilities. For example, they may decline a job interview, skip a class, or shut down during a mentoring session—not because they don't care, but because they are terrified of failing or being judged. Their trauma convinces them that it's safer to reject the opportunity outright than to risk the pain of disappointment or rejection.

This is why so many Dreamers from foster care or any young person struggle to value the resources and support available to them. It's not that they don't want to succeed; it's that their trauma has taught them that success is unattainable or temporary. They carry the weight of their past into every decision they make, and without intervention, they remain stuck in this cycle of self-doubt and avoidance.

Breaking the Cycle with SMART DREAMS

SMART DREAMS is more than just a concept—it's a therapeutic empowerment lifestyle designed to transform trauma into self-confidence, clarity of personal identity, and intentional decision-making. Breaking free from survival mode requires intentional effort and a support system that prioritizes healing and empowerment. Dreamers must first recognize the role trauma plays in their lives and understand that their fears and insecurities are not a reflection of their worth or potential. Awareness is crucial because, without it, they will continue to repeat patterns of avoidance and self-sabotage.

As mentors, caregivers, and advocates, we have a responsibility to create environments that foster this awareness and provide the tools needed for growth. It starts with building trust. Dreamers need to feel safe before they can begin to open about their experiences and aspirations. This means being patient, consistent, and empathetic in our approach. Remember, they've been let down before—by people, systems, and circumstances—so rebuilding trust takes time and intentionality.

Once trust is established, we can begin guiding them toward personal reflection and self-discovery. Encouraging Dreamers to identify their strengths and passions helps shift their focus from what they've endured to what they can achieve. This process also involves helping them establish core values and principles that will serve as a foundation for their decision-making. When Dreamers understand who they are and what they stand for, they are better equipped to navigate challenges and pursue opportunities with confidence.

Transforming Trauma into Triumph

The journey from surviving to thriving is not easy, but it is possible. *It begins with helping Dreamers understand that their trauma does not define them and that they have the power to rewrite their story. For many, their past experiences have instilled a mindset of self-preservation, where avoiding risks feels safer than striving for success. By addressing the underlying pain and providing consistent support, we can guide them toward a life where opportunities are embraced, not feared.

Dreamers are not broken—they are resilient. They carry within them the strength to overcome, the courage to grow, and the potential to achieve greatness. Our role is to help them see that and to provide the tools and encouragement they need to believe it for themselves. Together, we can transform trauma into triumph and create a future where every Dreamer no longer just survives but thrives–boldly and confidently pursuing their dreams.

SMART DREAMS empowers Dreamers to rewrite their narratives, turning their traumas into stepping stones for growth. It equips them with the confidence to build meaningful relationships, the resilience to face challenges, and the clarity to make decisions that align with their purpose.

*

Together, using the tools and strategies outlined in this book, we can create a future where every Dreamer you care for has the foundation to achieve their dreams. This isn't just about providing resources; it's about instilling the mindset and habits necessary for long-term success. SMART DREAMS is a transformative movement—one that ensures every Dreamer not only sees their potential but boldly steps into it, creating a legacy of resilience and empowerment for generations to come.

Introduction

At 18, I was stepping into a world I thought I was ready for because I already felt grown: adulthood. Aging out of foster care in Lake County, FL, I was determined to distance myself from everything that reminded me of "the system." The trauma I had endured while in care left me wanting to escape as far as possible from case managers and anyone associated with foster care. In my mind, if I had survived the system, surely, I could survive adulthood too. I imagine you've worked with plenty of Dreamers like that, right? For me to make that happen, I felt I had to say "forget the system" entirely, get a job, and start doing my own thing or find someone willing to let me stay with them. Unfortunately, like most kids aging out of foster care, I didn't have a way to make that happen at the time. So, I enrolled in a foster care program and decided to continue my education by attending Tallahassee Community College in Tallahassee, FL. When I enrolled in the foster care program to go to school full-time, I received a <u>monthly stipend</u> of $1,256 from the state that I used to pay my bills. After aging out at 18, I was already previously running away from my group home and promoting parties working in the nightlife scene, so I was comfortable being alone and on college campuses. However, when reflecting on the decision, I only chose school because I needed a way to pay my bills and I didn't want time taken away from partying and having fun as I was already doing on campus, so I chose the school route! Luckily, I chose a school a long way from my foster care agency, so all I had to do was submit a school schedule showing I was registered for the semester, monthly attendance, and grades at the end of every semester. At first, I was like, hell naw, my agency trying to control me and now I got to talk to a case manager again monthly, But because of my love for money and needing to survive at the time, I quickly realized a 1 time monthly conversation for $1,256 was not a bad conversation to have (laughing out loud). And if I made the conversation sound good enough, like I was handling my shit, then I wouldn't have to worry about talking so much on the next few meetings until it was time to submit my grades. Most Dreamer's aren't thinking like this, but hopefully, after reading this or learning from you reading it, they will. People always ask if I could tell the old me something, what would it be, well……

"Double up on your learning time and get paid to learn. Don't waste people's time and be real when updating them on your life, so you won't have to worry about them all on your back for things you really don't need. But if you ask for support and be stubborn how I was when aging out, then expect pushback and to be asked a lot of questions about why you need support (your monthly check). You only have 5 years to get help. That may seem like a long time but let me break it down for you in conversations. It really equals out to 60 conversations total with people who really want to see you win. So, make the best of them, not use them!"

Ok, now back to the story. So, as I succeeded in aging out and surviving life away from the system as far as I could, I failed to establish a foundation of values and principles that would set me up for success to thrive. I closed people out, tried to do my own thing, and lived life to the best of my ability. However, within 2 years, I blew through many relationships, experienced many failed opportunities, and made poor decisions that wasted my time and resources. Despite having all the resources and relationships I needed right in front of me, I found myself homeless by the age of 21 instead of being on a path to success. I ended up living in my car for 6 months sometimes going without showers or food, experiencing several embarrassing moments with poor hygiene, and having others offering up their home because of my smell and presentation until I decided to move back home. At this point, I ended up a statistic that I never knew was real until I became an advocate of foster care and saw that I was a part of a high-risk community. If you don't know about the statistics of young people aging out of foster care, then here are some often spoke about:

- **50% may be homeless within 18 months.**

- **25% may be arrested within 2 years.**

- **7 out of 10 girls may become pregnant before the age of 21.**

- **Less than 3% will be successful by the age of 23.**

So, with these statistics still facing our society today, this book is my personal view of principles I think professionals should use in their daily lives to work with Dreamer's with trauma. These principles build a foundation of success for Dreamers to excel socially, emotionally, mentally, physically, and spiritually, defy the current statistics of Dreamer's aging out of foster care systems across the world.

Part 1: SMART Builds Personal Connection!

Over the course of my life, learning to understand my trauma and emotions, I now realize trust, respect, & love are key to connection. It wasn't until a recent life experience that I learned that I could speak a good game and walk a good game but not provide a great experience to enjoy the game if you know what I mean. In other words, we can want to achieve having a connection with someone in a relationship, personally or professionally, but if we don't approach it SMART, then we may end up hurting the relationship before it can begin or be strengthened.

SMART is a motivational principle created to help professionals connect with Dreamers who have trauma in a therapeutic and empowering manner to establish a relationship. It's also a way we can educate Dreamers on how to apply when sharing their DREAMS, aspirations, or needs. SMART represents:

*

S: Specific

M: Motivating

A: Attentive

R: Relevant

T: Timing

SMART will establish trust when being specific and motivating, trust through being attentive and relevant, and love by considering the timing in their lives when delivering and connecting with them.

Because most of my life correlates to foster care, I will use my personal testimony and experiences to describe how I was not engaged accurately and how the system's efforts to keep me protected and safe really put me in survival mode, feeling alone and having to fight for my safety. When thinking of the SMART motivational principle to build a connection with your Dreamers, also think of SMART in your own life and how you share your needs and aspirations. If you practice it daily or every chance that presents itself, it will become a principle that allows you to get your aspirations, needs, or "DREAMS" out to the world in a specific and clear motivating way that makes people want to support and be involved as well as get Dreamers to trust, respect, and love you.

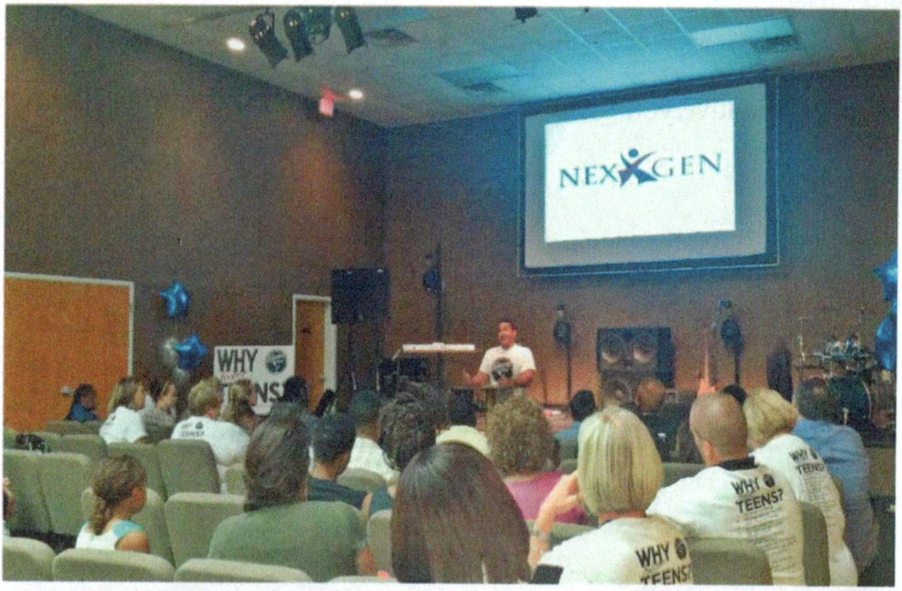
WHY TEENS?

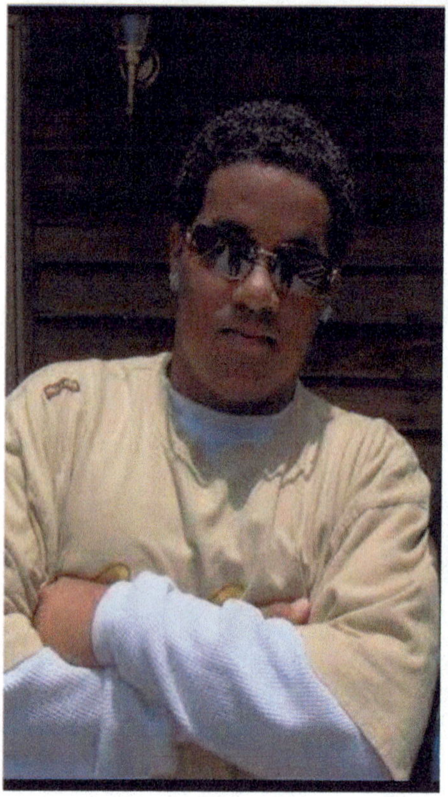

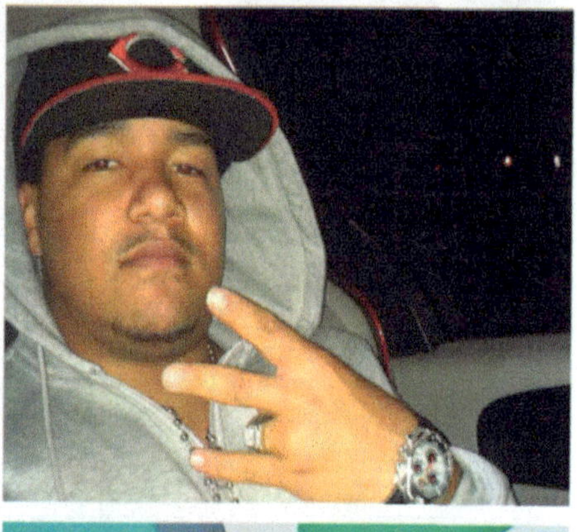

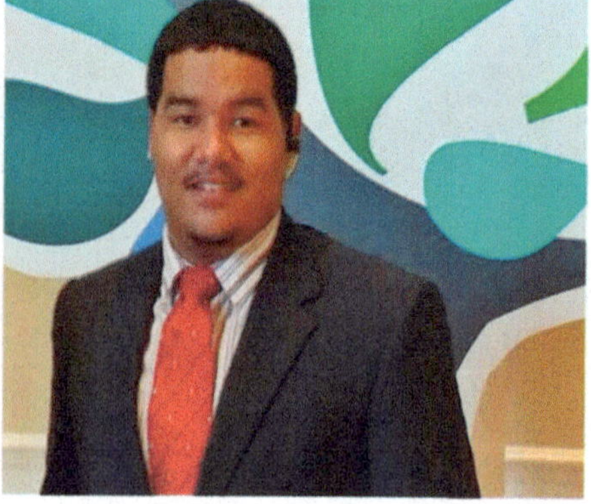

Introduction to Part One

I'm going to take you a little deeper into my journey. For those in the human services community, this story should resonate and serve as an immediate tool in your work. I'll share my experience of entering foster care and how "un-SMART" my case manager was—not literally, of course. She was well-educated, experienced, and genuinely caring. In fact, she was the one we turned to when my mother needed help protecting me. However, when I entered foster care, she didn't approach my life SMART, and as a result, she never truly connected with me to offer the support I needed.

You see, I entered the foster care system by choice—my mother's choice. She called the case manager who had previously worked with us (that's another story for another day) and asked if she could take me in because we were on the run, and she couldn't provide a stable home for me. Naturally, I was sad and upset but felt safe because I knew this case manager. Little did I know, I was about to enter a living hell, a prison I wouldn't escape from.

My mother and I met the case manager at the local foster care office. While they discussed the upcoming process, I played in a well-decorated room designed for kids, with TVs and game systems for teenagers. This was the "visitation room" where families meet with their children. Thank God for that room in offices today. Though I used to hate it, given my story, I now understand that it provides much-needed comfort to kids and their families. A big thank you to all the agencies that maintain these spaces!

After what felt like forever, it was time to say goodbye to my mother so she could get her life together, and we could be reunited. Before parting, the case manager sat us down and explained how the next few months would play out, including visitation schedules, guidelines for using the phone at the foster home to talk with my mother, and the possibility that it could take 6-12 months before I could go back home. My mother and I exchanged sad smiles, hugged each other tightly, and cried. As you might imagine that hug felt like the wrong decision, even though we knew it was the best one. After all, I was a mama's boy through and through.

My mom let go of me, and we walked towards the exit door hand in hand. She walked out, looked back, released my hand, and waved goodbye, crying as she walked to her car. The agency door closed, and I watched her drive off from the door with tears falling down my face. Little did I know, that would be the last time I ever saw my mother.

My case manager dropped me off at the first foster home, but it was only a temporary placement. I stayed there for one night, then moved to another home, and another, until I finally went through 7-10 different ones. Eventually, I landed in a home where I wouldn't hear from my case manager for the next 6-8 months. Despite call after unanswered call, she had no idea that I was being physically, emotionally, and verbally abused. This was the home where I began having suicidal thoughts, where I wished I had never existed, and where I started questioning my mother's decision to leave me. The way the foster parent treated me and the other kids, the way she allowed us to be beaten by other foster children, and the fact that my case manager never reached out to check on me—these experiences led me to a dark place I had never been before.

After about six months of this, the foster parent told me one night to pack my bags because the transporter was coming to get me for visitation and court the next morning. I asked her what was happening, and she just said, "Don't ask questions, just get your stuff and be ready, little boy." Now, let's take a moment to think about what you might imagine I was feeling as a 12-year-old kid at that moment.

1. Was I excited to leave the abusive situation?

2. Was I fearful of leaving one bad situation only to enter a potentially worse one?

3. Was I excited about possibly going home after nearly 6-8 months in the system?

If you answered #3, you're wrong. I felt all three emotions, but I was most hopeful for #3. The keyword here is "hopeful," which I know is a crucial feeling that drives us to make decisions for our lives. When someone loses hope for their future, they lose the energy to make decisions that move them forward. They're willing to settle for anything just to find some sense of satisfaction.

So yes, I was up all night, excited beyond belief, barely wanting to sleep. But it was a weeknight, so I had to get in bed and turn off the lights. I eventually dozed off. The next morning, the foster parent woke me up in her usual grouchy, cursing manner, but I didn't care. I heard nothing, saw nothing, and said nothing—just smiled and started getting ready to leave. I rushed to the front of the house and asked if the transporter was there yet. Of course, I got yelled at because they hadn't arrived, so I just sat at the table and waited.

It was around 6:30 a.m., still dark outside when I saw some lights coming down the street. I jumped up and ran to the window, only to watch the car zoom past the house. Disappointed, I sat back down. About 45 minutes later, after the scheduled pickup time, the transporter finally arrived. I grabbed my things and got in the car. As soon as we were on the road, I started asking questions, the main one being, "Where are we going?" The transporter responded, "We're going to court for a hearing with your mother and the judge." Now, mind you, I was

12 years old and didn't know what any of that meant, except for the part about "with your mother." So naturally, I thought option #3 was about to come true—I was going home!

I was ecstatic in the backseat, fidgeting with everything, talking the transporter's ear off, and being ignored, just happy to be out of that horrible foster home. In my head, I was on my way home. I sat there smiling, anticipating the moment I would see my mom again.

We arrived at the courthouse, and I jumped out of the car with all my trash bags. Yes, in the foster care system, most Dreamers travel from home to home with all their belongings in trash bags. Sadly, that's still the case today. But as I got out with my bags, the transporter told me to leave them in the car. I turned back, put them in the backseat, and accidentally slammed the door. Naturally, I got yelled at again. I didn't care; I was too focused on what was about to happen.

Once inside the courthouse, I became even more anxious and fidgety, asking repeatedly, "Where's my mommy?

Where's my mommy? Can I see her yet?" I looked at every short white woman with brown hair that passed by, hoping one of them was her. Following the transporter without getting any answers, we reached a large hallway with many doors. We walked to one door, and behind it was another hallway leading to what looked like a larger room. On the side was a small room with the door open, all white with a table, two chairs, another door on the opposite side, and a camera in the top corner. The transporter said, "You can go in there and have a seat."

I walked in, thinking my mother would be joining me. I sat down, still excited. Two minutes passed, then five, then ten, and finally, the door across the room opened. I jumped up but quickly realized it wasn't my mother. It was a large black man in a long black robe. I sat back down, tears welling up in my eyes, but the man smiled and said, "Hey, Michael, it's going to be okay. Is it fine if I call you Michael?" I nodded, not wanting to talk. The transporter had left by this point, so it was just me and him. Now, I know this was the judge, but back then, I didn't know who he was.

He began talking to me with such motivating energy and big smiles that I started to open up and smile back. I don't remember everything we talked about, but there was one question he asked me that I'll never forget. He said, "Michael, if there was anything you could have as a kid with your mother, what would it be?"

Before I tell you my answer, let me put my life at that time in perspective for you. I was 12 years old, in foster care because my mother was being chased by drug dealers, and we had been moving from home to home. I hadn't seen my mom in almost six months and missed her terribly. So, I responded, "I would love to go back home with my mom, see her every day, live in a nice home in one community so I can have the same friends, go to the same school, and just be a kid."

I thought that was the best answer I could give, and I sincerely believed it would help my mom. But apparently, it wasn't the right answer. The judge looked at me compassionately and said, "Well, Michael, because of your answer and the way I can see you love your mom very much, I'm going to have to terminate her parental rights in the state of Florida. You will no longer be going home to your mother or be able to see her again. The state will work to find you a family for adoption so that your wishes as a child can be fulfilled." Then within seconds, I heard my mother scream in what seemed to be the next room over, "Nooo. Today is the day you just killed me!"

When I tell you, I lost my s***, believe me. I jumped up from the chair and ran out the door, crying uncontrollably, screaming for my mother, "Mommy! Mommy!" The transporter grabbed me as I came through the door, tried to hold me, but I just pushed and shoved, trying to get free. At that moment, I didn't care about anyone; I just wanted to find my mother, but they wouldn't let me see her.

I ended up running down the hallway and into the courthouse lobby, then out the front doors. As I reached the parking lot, I looked around frantically for my mom's car, but it was nowhere to be found. She wasn't there. Then the transporter caught up to me, grabbed me, and pulled me back inside.

She sat me down and said, "Michael, your mom's not coming. You cannot see her anymore."

Now, I was in full-blown hyperventilation mode. She had me sit down, gave me some water, and I just sat there crying with no one around, while the transporter stood off to the side watching me. Eventually, I looked up and saw the judge walking down the hallway towards me. I stood up and ran over, trying to hit him, asking him why he did this to me. The transporter intervened and held me back while the judge kept saying, "It's okay, Michael. I'm doing this for your protection. You'll understand when you're older." But at that moment, I just hated him and wished I had never spoken to him.

About two hours later, I was still in a daze, just numb. I wasn't sure what had happened, but I knew I wouldn't be going home. The transporter took me to the car and said we were going back to the foster home. I didn't even care at that point; I had no emotion left. I was like a zombie, numb to the world.

For the next two years, I went through approximately 40 different foster homes and had at least three different case managers. Eventually, I had the opportunity to begin the adoption process, but it fell through—that's a story for another day. My point in sharing this with you is to illustrate how critical it is to approach situations with a SMART mindset, especially when it comes to dealing with children in the foster care system and/or with trauma. We must be strategic, empathetic, and attentive to the emotional needs of these kids. In my case, despite the good intentions, the lack of a SMART approach led to years of emotional turmoil that could have been avoided.

Chapter 1: (S)pecific
"Don't beat around the bush"

Dreamers, especially those who have endured traumatic experiences, often have short attention spans and a heightened sensitivity to how they are communicated. This means they require clear, direct communication that leaves no room for ambiguity. Being open and honest is not just a courtesy—it's a necessity. When dealing with Dreamers who have been through significant emotional and psychological pain, as I have in my own journey, trust is fragile. They are already struggling to believe in the intentions of adults, particularly professionals who are supposed to be in their corner. If you fail to be specific or try to soften the truth by being vague, you risk them feeling disrespected or undervalued, which can quickly lead to them disengaging or reacting negatively.

*

CHAPTER 1: (S)PECIFIC — "DON'T BEAT AROUND THE BUSH"

Reflect on this: What does being specific mean to you?

_____

_____

_____

In my own story, I encountered multiple instances where the professionals responsible for my well-being failed to provide clear, specific guidance. Instead of helping, this lack of clarity caused confusion and frustration and ultimately led to mistrust and resentment. When the professionals supporting you don't communicate directly, it feels like they are hiding something or underestimating your ability to handle the truth. This can be particularly damaging for Dreamers, who are already dealing with feelings of insecurity and inadequacy.

*

CHAPTER 1: (S)PECIFIC — "DON'T BEAT AROUND THE BUSH"

Share examples in which the professionals could have done better by being specific.

_____

_____

_____

When you are not specific, you leave Dreamers to fill in the gaps themselves, which can be dangerous, as their minds might wander to the worst-case scenarios or false assumptions. For example, if a young adult is facing a significant change, such as transitioning into a new home or school, they need to know exactly what to expect. Vague reassurances like "It will all work out" or "Don't worry about it" are not helpful. Instead, they need concrete information: what the new environment will be like, who they will be living with, what the rules are, and how they will be supported during the transition.

Additionally, being specific helps to empower Dreamers by making them an active participant in their own life plan. It gives them a sense of control in a situation where they often feel powerless. When you *clearly outline expectations, goals, and the steps needed to achieve

CHAPTER 1: (S)PECIFIC   "DON'T BEAT AROUND THE BUSH"

them, you are not just informing them—you are equipping them with the tools they need to succeed. Specificity fosters accountability, both on the part of Dreamers and adults, creating a partnership built on mutual respect and understanding.

What are some ways you can be specific with your Dreamers?

_____

_____

_____

You see, at the end of the day, as adults, we sometimes get caught up in our roles as authority figures or mentors, and we might think that withholding certain information or sugarcoating the truth is in the best interest of Dreamers. We might believe that by being vague, we are protecting them from potential pain or disappointment. However, this approach often backfires. Instead of building trust, it erodes it, leading to feelings of resentment and a lack of trust. Dreamers are perceptive, and they can sense when something is being withheld. This not only damages the relationship but also undermines their confidence in you

CHAPTER 1: (S)PECIFIC — "DON'T BEAT AROUND THE BUSH"

as a reliable source of support.

In my experience, if my case manager had been more specific with me, it could have significantly altered my experience within the system. Dreamer's, particularly those aged 15 and older, need to be given clear, actionable steps that align with their personal DREAMS. If, for example, a young adult has fallen behind in school due to circumstances beyond their control, they shouldn't be forced into a traditional educational path that doesn't consider their unique situation. Instead, professionals should work with employment partners to create opportunities that allow them to earn money, receive professional development, and continue their education in a way that is manageable and meaningful to them.

What steps will you take to change your communication to be more specific?

-
-

*

On the other hand, if the young adult is thriving in a full-time school environment, they should be offered opportunities that align with their long-term goals, rather than just activities designed to keep them occupied or reward good behavior. How you communicate and support a young adult with a trauma background is critical. If you're not careful, they may become manipulative, especially if they feel that things are being handed to them without clear expectations or goals. While compassion and love are important, they are not the initial keys to connecting with a young adult who has experienced trauma. This kind of support can be intimidating at first, as it may remind them of the unhealthy ways their parents showed love. Therefore, be specific and always keep it real—there's no need to beat around the bush.

*

Chapter 2: (M)otivating
"Prepare your tone and body"

This might be one of the most critical steps in the SMART sequence, yet it's often overlooked or used incorrectly by professionals. Motivating words and body language are essential every time you plan to engage with Dreamer's. Before you even begin the conversation, think about keywords that align with your topic of discussion, and prepare your body language and tone to be positive, uplifting, and forward-thinking—especially if you're delivering bad news or information the young adult may not want to hear.

Reflect on this: **Do you remember that one teacher who was always monotone or had the same dull approach every day?** They were the ones you dreaded attending their class and maybe even considered skipping or dropping their class. We all had someone like that at some point in our lives. You don't want to be that person for your Dreamers.

*

CHAPTER 2: (M)OTIVATING   "PREPARE YOUR TONE AND BODY"

In my story, there were numerous occasions where the relationships between my professionals and me could have been much stronger if they had used better words, tone, and body language. To be honest, at that time in my life, I wasn't particularly sensitive to what people said I had become somewhat numb to it. So, when professionals were yelling or talking down to me, I didn't really care. But thinking "SMART," they should have approached the situation differently.

List some examples of how you think the professionals working with me could have done better and more motivational.

_____

_____

_____

The way you communicate—both in words and in body language—matters immensely. Being "dry," or unengaging, can lead to disconnect and missed opportunities to build trust. It's not just about what you say, it's about how you say it. A monotone voice or indifferent posture can convey disinterest or lack of empathy, which

CHAPTER 2: (M)OTIVATING   "PREPARE YOUR TONE AND BODY"

can be incredibly damaging to a Dreamer who is already vulnerable.

What does be motivating mean to you?

_____

_____

_____

So, how can you avoid being dry with your Dreamer's? Start by consciously preparing your tone and body language before each interaction. Make sure your words are encouraging, and your posture is open and inviting. Your tone should reflect genuine care and a desire to see them succeed. Remember, motivation isn't just about the words you use—it's about the energy and sincerity behind them.

How can you avoid being dry with your Dreamer's?

_____

_____

_____

*

CHAPTER 2: (M)OTIVATING   "PREPARE YOUR TONE AND BODY"

Now, think about the steps you can take to change your communication style to be more motivating. It might involve practicing in front of a mirror, role-playing with a colleague, or simply being more mindful in your interactions. Whatever it takes, the goal is to ensure that your words and body language consistently convey motivation and support.

What steps are you going to take to change your communication to be more motivating?

_____

_____

_____

Now that you've gained perspective on the importance of not beating around the bush and being motivating in your interactions with Dreamers, let's consider the outcomes. If you apply these principles consistently in your conversations, you'll begin to earn their trust. Being direct while maintaining a motivating approach can go a long way in building relationships with Dreamers, many of whom may not have ever experienced a *trusting relationship with an adult*.

Trust is something we all value deeply, right? So, put yourself in their shoes—think about when you were their age, but also consider the real-life experiences documented in the Dreamer's case file. Reflect on how trust has been shaped by their past relationships. Now, use that insight and apply the SMART principles when engaging with them. You'll likely see your relationships with Dreamer's blossom in ways you hadn't imagined.

*

Chapter 3: (A)ttentive
"Pay attention"

Now that you've learned how to gain the trust of your Dreamers, let's delve deeper into the next crucial phase: Respect. Trust opens the door—it's what earns you that friendly "What's up, Miss or Mr. [insert name]" every time your Dreamers see you. But cultivating respect? That's where true connection begins. Respect allows your Dreamers to open up about their day, feelings, or emotions in those follow-up conversations. It's what makes them comfortable sharing their deepest thoughts and experiences with you.

To foster this respect, it's essential that your Dreamers feel heard, seen, and in control during interactions. Using the term "advised" rather than "told" can significantly impact how they perceive your intent. Advising suggests collaboration and respect for their autonomy, which is foundational in building trust.

*

What does giving your full attention mean to you?

_____

_____

_____

Truly attending to your Dreamers means creating a space where they feel they have your undivided focus. SMART conversations require time and should never feel rushed or secondary to other tasks. If a Dreamer approaches you with a concern or a thought, it's pivotal to pause what you're doing and confirm whether they need your complete attention. This act alone can reinforce their significance to you and solidify their respect in your relationship.

List some examples of how you could do a better job of giving your full attention:

_____

_____

_____

CHAPTER 3: (A)TTENTIVE   "PAY ATTENTION"

A common pitfall for many professionals is trying to conduct meaningful interactions while distracted, such as during a professional car ride or in the middle of a task. This split focus not only reduces the quality of communication but also signals to Dreamers that they are a secondary priority, which can dilute the trust and respect you've worked to establish.

What are some ways you will give your full attention when engaging with your Dreamers?

_____

_____

_____

Being fully present in your interactions communicates intention and care, laying a strong foundation for respect. This attentiveness shows Dreamers that their voice matters and that you are genuinely interested in their well-being and personal growth.

*

What steps will you take to change your communication to be more attentive?

_____

_____

_____

Enhancing your attentiveness not only improves your interactions but also strengthens the overall relationship. It demonstrates that you are truly invested in their success and happiness, which can significantly impact how they engage with you and the world around them.

Chapter 4: (R)elevant
"Make it make sense"

In the previous chapter, we explored the importance of being attentive. But being attentive goes beyond simply choosing the right time to have a conversation or engaging with your Dreamers with focus. It's also about truly understanding their feelings, current life circumstances, and what makes them happy and fulfilled. This deeper level of attentiveness allows you to connect with your Dreamers in ways that are not just respectful but also relevant to their dreams and aspirations.

To build respect and have a meaningful impact in your relationship with your Dreamers, it's essential that every important conversation or accountability measure ties back into their dreams and how it is relevant to their future. If Dreamers don't feel that their life circumstances are being considered, they may shut down, rebel, or disengage by looking at their phone or avoiding eye contact. Your job is to make the conversation meaningful to them by showing how it directly relates to their goals and aspirations.

*

CHAPTER 4: (R)ELEVANT — "PAY ATTENTION"

Based on my personal story, list some examples of how you think the professionals could have done better by communicating relevant information in my life:

_____
_____
_____

What does communicating relevant information mean to you?

_____
_____
_____

What are some ways you will begin to communicate relevant information with your Dreamers?

_____
_____
_____

HAPTER 4: (R)ELEVANT   "PAY ATTENTION"

What steps are you going to take to change your communication to be relevant?

_____

_____

_____

When working with a young adult, especially in a role like that of a case manager or child welfare professional, you must deliver a vast amount of information and services. This includes not just logistical information but also emotional guidance that can transform a Dreamer's perspective of themselves and their future. Your approach should not just focus on checking off boxes but also on making information and services relevant to their personal goals.

For example, when discussing court and transition planning at 16, don't just focus on checking off the boxes for housing, education, medical care, and other essentials. Instead, start by asking the young adult what they want to accomplish in life. Then, explain how their choices in housing will be crucial for achieving that goal, how selecting the right educational path will support them financially, and how all these elements are interconnected to help them enjoy life and invest in their dreams. The key is to deliver the information in a way that makes sense to them by tying it into their DREAMS.

In Part 2 of this book, we will dive deeper into how everything we do in our work should make sense to the young adult and align with their DREAMS if we are communicating it correctly. The more relevant you can make your conversations and guidance, the more likely it is that your Dreamers will stay engaged and motivated on their journey while also respecting you for your time and commitment to supporting them.

Chapter 5: (T)iming
"It's not about you"

Timing is the most critical factor when engaging with Dreamers. While trust and respect are equally important, love is the ultimate goal. It's not just about the casual "What's up, Miss or Mr. [insert name]" or your Dreamers opening up about their day, feelings, or emotions. It's about those moments when you make a mistake or are tired and can't fully show up for them. In those moments, they won't lash out or hold it against you; instead, they will trust your word, respect your voice, and love you regardless.

To foster this love, you must be mindful of timing and always pay attention to their body language, moods, and overall engagement. These often indicate the right moments for meaningful interaction. Dreamers do not respond well to being pressured, caught off guard, or approached without time to prepare for the conversation.

*

What does be sensitive to timing mean to you?

_____

_____

_____

If you're making an initial connection with a Dreamer, it's your responsibility to create an environment that fosters open conversation or presents an opportunity to ask some introductory questions or comments.

Avoid being the case manager or professional who interrupts Dreamers during school activities or hobbies they enjoy. Imagine being deeply engaged in an activity you love, only to be pulled aside to discuss personal matters, disrupting your focus and potentially your emotional state. Such interruptions can significantly affect a Dreamer's ability to engage and may even lead to feelings of frustration or resentment.

*

List some examples in which you think the professionals could have been more sensitive to timing:

_____

_____

_____

Moreover, if a Dreamer expresses frustration or react negatively during such interruptions, they risk being labeled as challenging or misbehaved. This labeling can affect how they are treated by new staff or any adult they encounter within the system, perpetuating a cycle of mistrust and misunderstanding.

Timing is not just about choosing the right moment; it's about being empathetic to the Dreamer's current emotional and mental state. By syncing your discussions with moments when Dreamers feel safe and receptive, you not only respect their current state but also significantly enhance the effectiveness of your communication.

*

CHAPTER 5: (T)IMING   "IT'S NOT ABOUT YOU"

What are some ways you can be more intentional with your timing when engaging with your Dreamers?

_____

_____

_____

This thoughtful approach to timing goes a long way in building a trusting relationship. It shows that you are not just there to supervise or manage them but to support them in a way that respects their space and honors their pace. Such sensitivity to timing confirms to Dreamers that you are genuinely interested in their well-being and dedicated to helping them achieve their dreams without adding unnecessary stress to their lives.

Therefore, when it's time to engage and deliver information that ties into their DREAMS, careful planning of the timing, location, and energy of your interactions is essential. This approach ensures that the exchange of information is productive and respectful, fostering a positive relationship between you and your Dreamers.

*

CHAPTER 5: (T)IMING — "IT'S NOT ABOUT YOU"

What steps will you take to change your communication to be intentional with timing?

_____

_____

_____

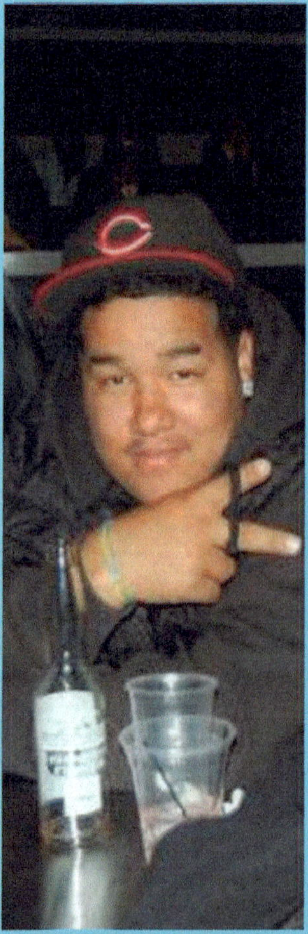

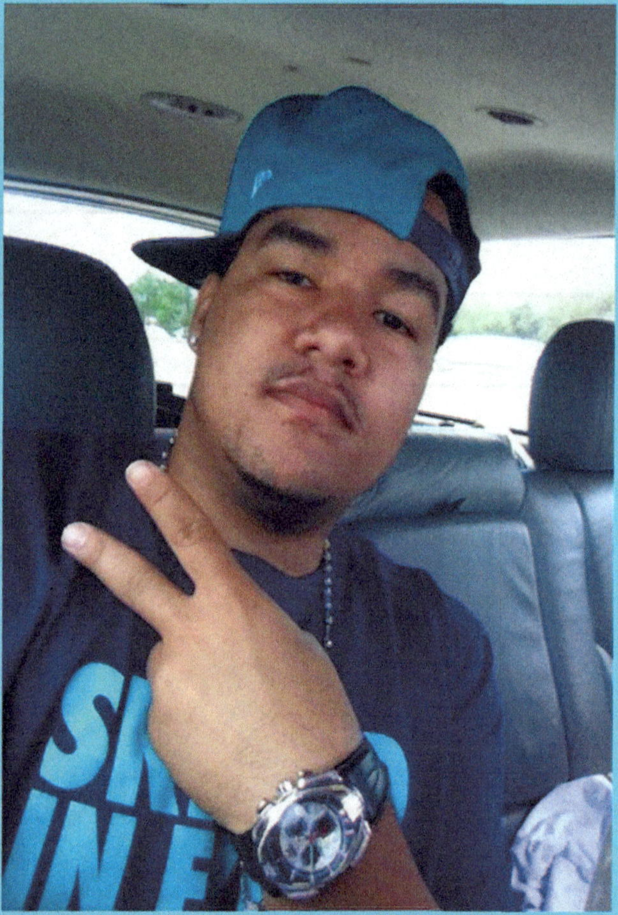

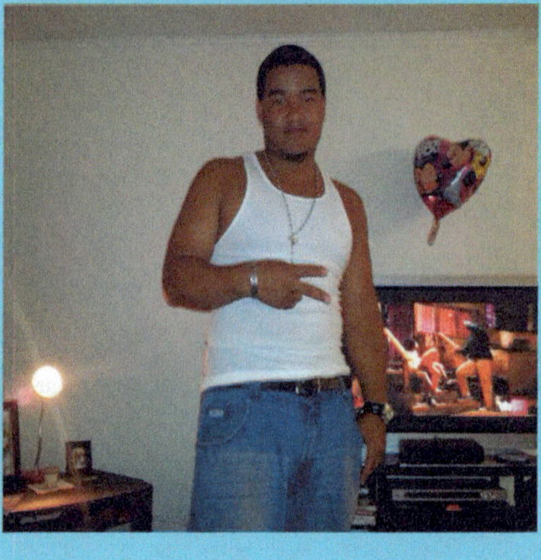

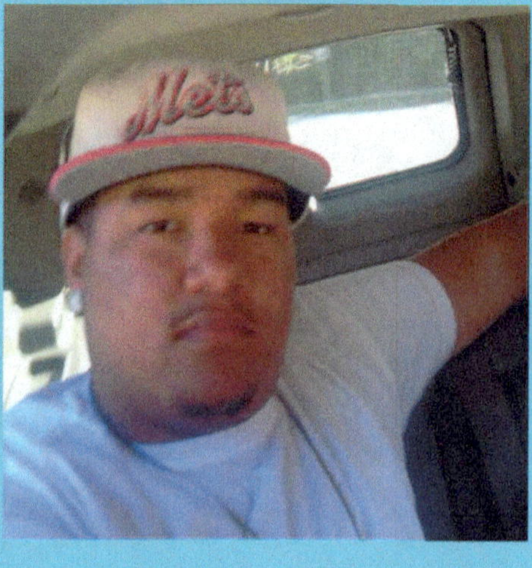
Mets

Part 2: DREAMS Build Self-Confidence!

In Part 1, we explored how to be SMART in establishing connections with your Dreamers to build meaningful relationships. Now, as we transition into Part 2, the question arises: once you've made that connection, how do you get them to value the wisdom, resources, and services you are offering? We all remember how, in our youth, we often resisted listening to parents or adults who tried to guide us. This resistance can be even stronger for those who have experienced trauma, making them feel skeptical of advice from others.

Part 2 of this handbook introduces the DREAMS Mindset principles, designed to help Dreamers transition from dependency to a state of self-reliance and confidence. These principles are not just about providing support; they're about empowering Dreamers to see and cultivate their potential through a framework that respects their personal relationships, experiences, and aspirations.

The DREAMS Mindset includes:

- **Personal Identity:** Encouraging Dreamers to define themselves on their own terms.

- **Self-Confidence:** Building trust in their habits, abilities, and decisions.

- **Self-Motivation:** Inspiring a drive from within to pursue their goals.

- **High-Level Mindset:** Elevating their thinking to plan and act strategically.

- **Life Purpose:** Helping them discover and pursue meaningful life goals.

The implementation of the DREAMS framework provides a success plan encompassing:

1. **D – Driver:** Teaching Dreamers to take control of their lives.
   - Vision Planning: Mapping out future aspirations.
   - Personal Values: Identifying what is most important to them.
   - Goal Setting: Establishing clear, actionable objectives.

2. **R – Relationships:** Cultivating a network of supportive, safe relationships.

    - Support: Family and therapists who offer emotional backing.
    - Accountability: Coaches and mentors who guide and challenge.
    - Faith: Spiritual advisors who provide moral and existential guidance.
    - Entertainment: Friends and associates who offer relaxation and social interaction.

3. **E – Education:** Promoting a sophisticated mindset through learning.

    - Social-Emotional: Developing skills to manage emotions and relationships.
    - Mental: Enhancing intellectual capacity and critical thinking.
    - Financial: Understanding and managing personal finances.

4. **A – Accountability:** Emphasizing the importance of personal responsibility.

    - o Personal Ownership: Taking responsibility for personal choices.
    - o Personal Organization: Maintaining order in personal and professional life.
    - o Personal Reflection: Engaging in regular self-assessment and adaptation.

5. **M – Motivation:** Discovering and nurturing personal 'why.'

    - o Vision Board: Visualizing goals and dreams.
    - o Affirmations: Reinforcing positive self-talk and beliefs.
    - o Daily Routine: Establishing consistent habits that promote success.

6. **S – Spirituality:** Exploring deeper life purpose and values.

    - o Life Purpose: Identifying overarching goals and reasons for being.

- Prayer/Meditation Routine: Engaging in practices that promote reflection and peace.
- Servant Leadership: Leading by example and serving others.

By integrating these elements, the DREAMS Mindset not only aligns with the goals you aim to achieve with your Dreamers but also makes those goals relevant and attainable for them. This approach instills habits that lead to productivity, purpose, and personal satisfaction, laying a foundation for a fulfilling and exceptional life.

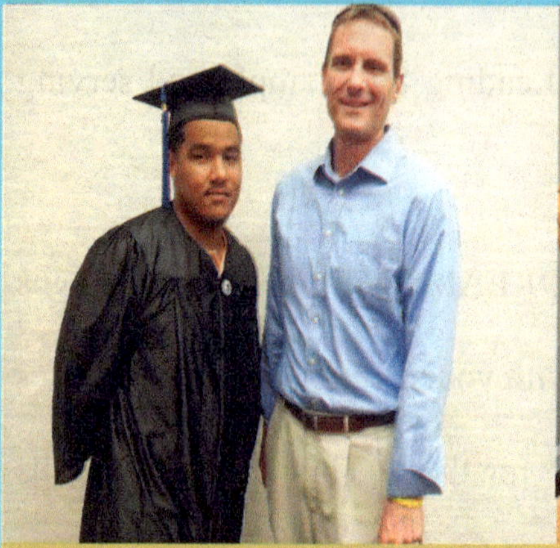

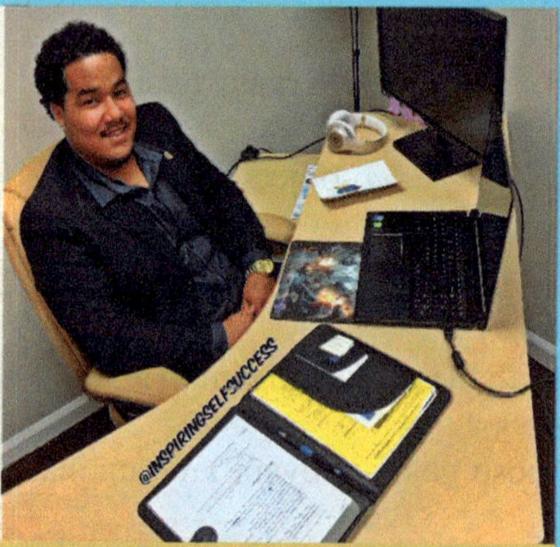
@INSPIRINGSELFSUCCESS

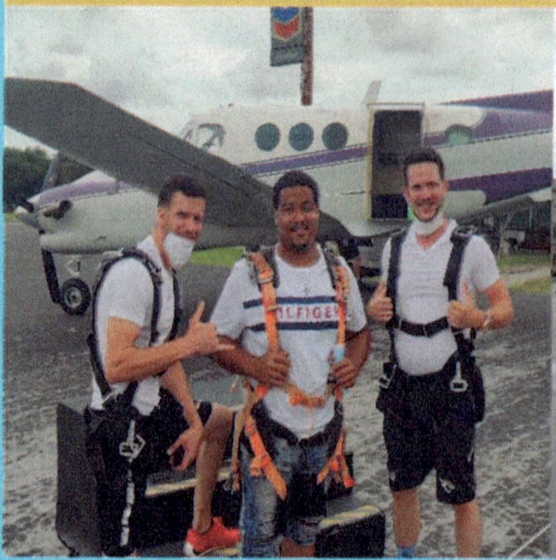

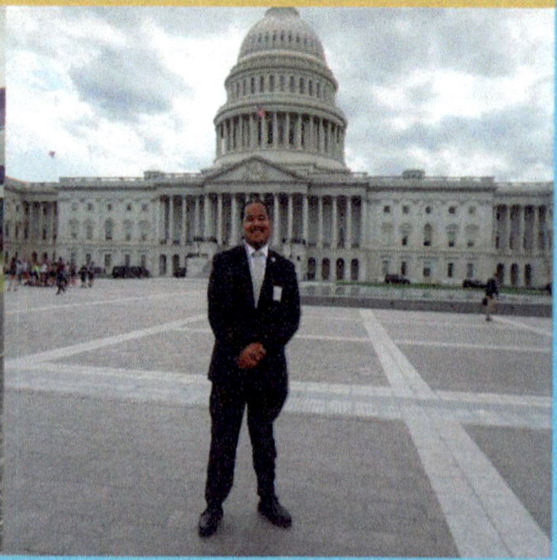

Introduction to Part Two

The DREAMS Mindset is built on achieving goals across several pivotal life areas:

1. Personal Identity (Confidence): Encouraging Dreamers to define themselves on their own terms and trust in their habits, abilities, and decisions.

2. Permanent Relationships (Family): Dreamers will learn the true meaning of family (SAFE Team), identify who belongs in their circle, and understand the habits necessary to nurture these relationships.

School Boy

3. Self-Sufficient Income (Career): Dreamers will envision a career that not only supports their desired lifestyle but also prepares them for success in the professional world.

4. Life Purpose (Spirituality): Dreamers will discover the importance of spirituality in defining their legacy and understanding what they truly represent in the world.

5. Bucket List (Travel/Fun): Dreamers will be encouraged to dream big, planning exciting activities and life experiences

they wish to accomplish.

6. Generational Wealth (Investments/Savings): Dreamers will learn about building and managing wealth that not only benefits them but also future generations.

Reflecting on my journey from foster care to adulthood highlights the critical importance of these goals. Looking back, I now know I could have achieved success much earlier if I had developed these skills and surrounded myself with a supportive, accountable SAFE team. That realization led me to stop blaming the system and instead take ownership of my future. I recognized that success wasn't just about the resources available to me, but about how I chose to use them. Once I stopped looking outward for blame, I found the strength to look inward for solutions.

So, my journey began with enrolling back into the foster care programs available to me, in which one included offering college support services while re-enrolling back into school. Apart of these services was being assigned a mentor. My mentor assigned to me was Matt McKibbin.

His role in my life was monumental. More than just education and guidance, he offered unwavering support, embodying the principles of SMART DREAMS. A lot of people think when working with Dreamers in foster care, it's just about how the mentor/professional connects with them, but that's only halfway. It's also about how the Dreamer connects with the mentor/professional and gives them a chance to be trusted. Our relationship wasn't just about Matt mentoring me—it was about me allowing myself to trust, to be open, and to embrace growth. True progress requires a two-way street; mentoring is as much about how the Dreamer responds as it is about how the mentor shows up.

Our first meeting didn't go as planned. Matt and I relationship started off rocky in the beginning with connecting, but not because of him, because he was trying and doing everything right, it was because of me. And as a society we need to acknowledge that. Sometimes it's not the professional fault because progress isn't being made, it is the Dreamers. For example, when I got a message from the program director that she found my mentor and I needed to come to her office at a certain time to meet him, I first thought, "damn, I thought it was just going to be another thing the system forgot about and let me slide by on without having one". But I respond, I will be there. Upon entering the director's office, I immediately see a guy sitting at her meeting table while she was sitting at her desk. I knod my head at him and walk over to her desk and begin talking. After I stop, she says, "Mike, meet Matt, the guy I mentioned about being your mentor". I look at her, look at him, then back at her and say "hell naw, Miss, me and him have nothing in common. He is an old white man who wouldn't know anything about how to help me with my life". So, I turned around and then began walking towards her office door. She stops me and then goes on to say, "Mike, you should at least give him a chance". Aggravated, I turn around and say ok, what's up Mr. Matt. From then on it was history. Although Matt had to be very patient. I was skeptical and dismissive, unable to see beyond our apparent differences. But Matt's greatest strength was his refusal to take things personally. He saw the potential behind my defensive attitude, and through his patience and persistence, he built the trust we both needed to move forward. Weekly meetings in the college cafeteria, personalized support, and eventually, invitations to family dinners became integral to my growth.

For someone like me, coming from a foster care background, those family dinners were more than just meals. They were moments of belonging—of being part of something stable and real. Experiences like these can either trigger or transform, and for me, they did both. Seriously, having a mentor or someone you care about invite you over for a dinner with their family, especially if they have little kids……can be triggering because you don't have your own family there or don't know how to respond if everyone is treating you nice. And then on the other hand, it can transform you into valuing those moments and inspired to recreate the same for yourself. Matt helped me realize that a true SAFE team— relationships that provides emotional, social, and practical support—was not just an idea but a reality within my reach. The DREAMS principles have been pivotal in my journey towards resilience. By establishing a vision and aligning with a purpose, we can shield ourselves from the lows of emotional, mental, and spiritual challenges, setting a course for a fulfilled and purposeful life.

SKYDIVE SPACE CENTER.com
THE WORLD'S HIGHEST JUMP AT 18,000 FEET!!!
SKYDIVE TODAY!!!
323-0016
HILFIGER

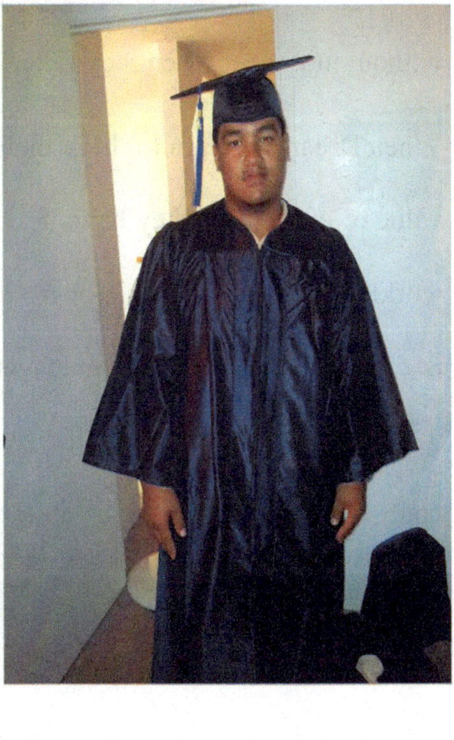

Chapter 6: (D)river
"Let them drive!"

Letting your Dreamers take the driver's seat might seem scary and risky, but it's essential for their development. Often, Dreamers might seem directionless, living life influenced by social pressures and sometimes unhealthy relationships. To shift their mindset and behaviors toward productivity, they need the freedom to make their own choices and be the primary navigators of their lives. The critical aspect here is your support—being there to guide and coach them without judgment when they falter.

When Dreamers learn to drive their life, they begin to appreciate the value of everything they have. For case managers and foster parents working with Dreamer's in or from foster care, this perspective shift is crucial. Typically, case managers focus on reunifying Dreamers with their families or finding them permanent foster homes, managing court cases, enrolling them in school, and coordinating health care and counseling as needed. However, while these are important, they often overshadow the Dreamer's most vital goals—their DREAMS.

CHAPTER 6: (D)RIVER "LET THEM DRIVE"

Instead of prioritizing logistical tasks, start discussions with Dreamers about their aspirations. Understand what support they need to achieve their DREAMS. This approach not only helps in finding a foster home that supports their ambitions but also fosters a more genuine relationship between Dreamers and foster families. It ensures that the placement is aligned not just with logistical needs but with personal growth and development goals.

Consider this: A home is identified to support a specific goal, motivating the foster parents to pay attention to the Dreamer's desires, making everything relevant to them, and choosing the right timing for support because the Dreamer was involved in the decision.

Now, as Dreamer's form their vision and goals, it's crucial to assess their processing patterns and perspectives. Do they have healthy values that promote happiness, or are their values skewed towards pleasing friends or romantic partners? It's vital to help them establish strong personal values because, without them, their vision and goals will constantly be sidelined by fleeting excitement or momentary pleasures.

*

Here are three habits you must teach your Dreamers to help them become the drivers of their lives and live confidently:

1. **Vision**:
    - Set at least one goal in each of the following areas, as previously mentioned:
        - Permanent Relationships
        - Self-Sufficient Income
        - Life Purpose
        - Bucket List
        - Generational Wealth
2. **Values**:
    - Learn to develop personal values that forge their identity. Initially, the DREAMS framework can serve as their identity foundation until they define their own.
    - Identify their social-emotional strengths and weaknesses.
    - Learn to establish clear boundaries.

3. **Goals**:

    o Understand what SMART goal setting is and how it applies to their DREAMS.

    o Practice setting SMART goals weekly, monthly, annually, and as needed to achieve self-sufficiency and financial security.

By empowering Dreamers to take control of their journey, you enable them to build a life that is not only about surviving but thriving. This approach encourages them to invest deeply in their futures, making informed choices that align with their long-term aspirations.

Chapter 7: (R)elationships
"Define their SAFE team!"

Understanding the influence of a Dreamer's environment and relationships is crucial for their success. Most Dreamers, especially those from challenging backgrounds, are profoundly affected by the dynamics around them. They often navigate their relationships based on survival instincts, which can lead to misinterpretations and unrealistic expectations. This is why it's essential to empower them to set the standard for how they view, build, and manage these relationships.

While in foster care, I had significantly flawed perceptions of the roles of the people around me:

- **Case Manager:** I thought they controlled every aspect of my life, including my family's stability and my future.

- **Foster Parent:** I viewed them merely as temporary caretakers, not as potential supporters or part of my extended family.

- **Group Home:** It seemed like a place for those who were unwanted or had nowhere else to go.

- **Case Manager Supervisor:** I believed their only role was to oversee my court hearings and not be involved in my day-to-day life.

- **Guardian Ad Litem:** They appeared as just sympathetic figures offering consolation gifts, not as advocates.

- **Therapist:** I mistakenly believed they were there to medicate rather than support me, to control rather than understand me.

This flawed perception highlights the critical need for Dreamers to accurately define and manage their relationships. If left unchecked, Dreamers can carry these misjudgments into adulthood, influencing how they interact in personal and professional capacities, often to their detriment.

The Importance of a SAFE Team

Every Dreamer, especially those transitioning out of foster care, should establish a **SAFE Team**—a dedicated group of individuals committed to supporting their journey towards self-sufficiency. This team plays a vital role in educating, developing, and ensuring a nurturing environment for Dreamers. By compartmentalizing their relationships, Dreamers can build a support network that genuinely understands and caters to their needs, helping them to feel secure, valued, and understood.

Components of a SAFE Team:

1. **(S)upport Members:**

    o **Role:** These individuals provide emotional support, celebrate special occasions, and meet personal needs. They are the emotional backbone of the Dreamer's network.

    o **Members:** Family, case manager, best friends.

2. **(A)ccountability Members:**

    o **Role:** They hold Dreamers accountable, offer constructive feedback, and keep them focused on their goals. This role is crucial for maintaining the Dreamer's progress and adherence to their personal development plans.

    o **Members:** Coaches, mentors, therapists.

3. **(F)aith Members:**

    - **Role:** Offer spiritual support, help find inner strength and connect with personal values. They provide a moral compass and a deeper sense of purpose.
    - **Members:** Pastors, priests, spiritual leaders.

4. **(E)ntertainment Members:**

    - **Role:** They bring joy and fun, organizing activities and events that allow for relaxation and building lasting memories. They ensure that the Dreamer's life balances work and play.
    - **Members:** Family, friends, associates.

Building the SAFE Team

To effectively support a Dreamer, each member of the SAFE Team should understand their role and its impact on the Dreamer's development. This understanding is crucial for fostering an atmosphere of trust, empathy, and mutual respect.

Engagement Strategies:

- **Workshops and Meetings:** Regularly scheduled meetings can help ensure all members of the SAFE team are on the same page and understand their roles.

- **Continuous Training:** Providing ongoing training and resources to team members can help them stay effective and empathetic in their roles.

Reflect on This:

- How can you, as a mentor or supporter, help Dreamers identify and establish a robust SAFE Team?

- What strategies can you employ to ensure that each member of the SAFE Team understands their role and contributes positively to the Dreamer's growth?

CHAPTER 7: (R)ELATIONSHIPS — "DEFINE THEIR SAFE TEAM"

By empowering Dreamers to define and manage their relationships strategically, you enable them to build a support system that not only meets their immediate needs but also supports their long-term growth and success. This approach ensures that Dreamers have the tools and support necessary to navigate life confidently, overcome challenges, and achieve their dreams.

*

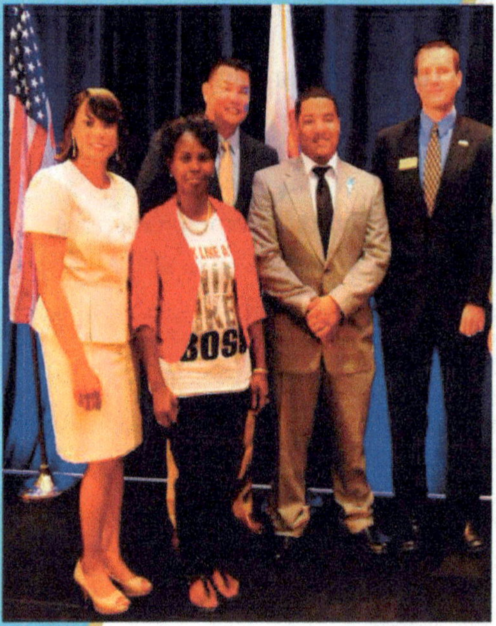

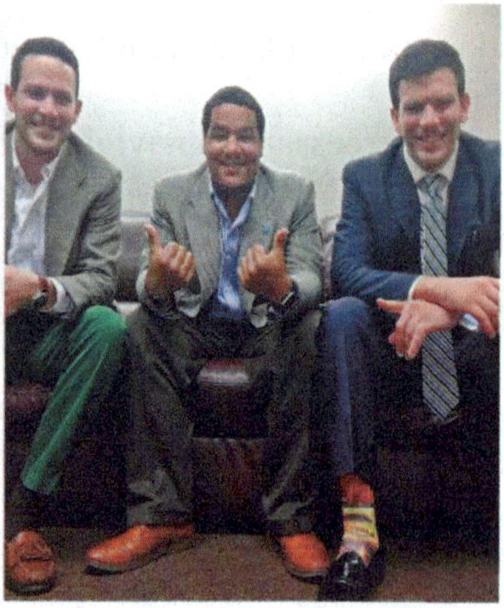

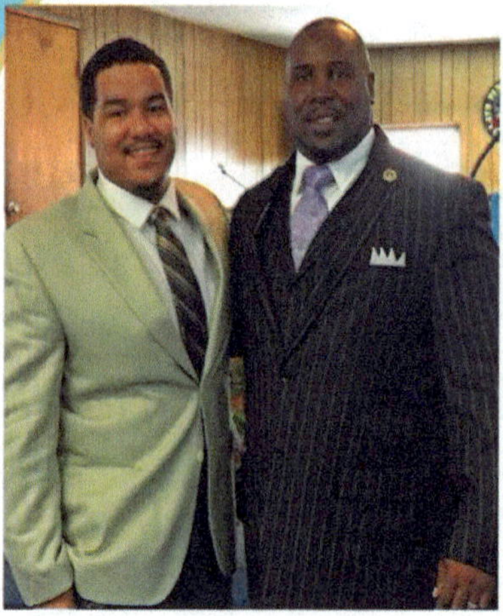

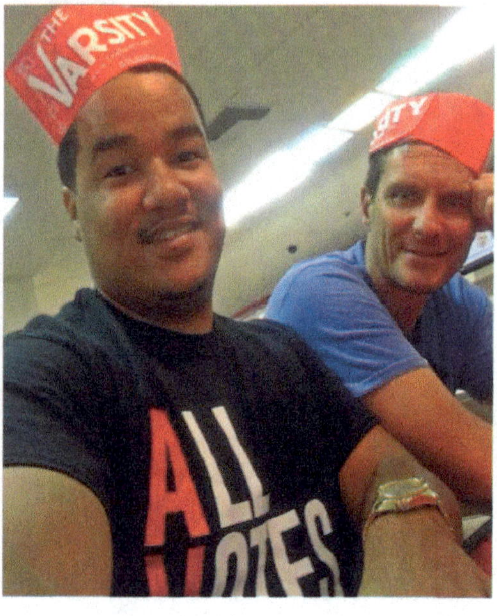
THE VARSITY

Chapter 8: (E)ducation
"Elevate their mindset!"

Education extends far beyond the classroom—it is the foundation of knowledge about the world around us and equips Dreamers with the tools to transform their environments into something better. Education fosters a unique perspective on life, helping Dreamer's form opinions and viewpoints on a vast array of subjects. It's not just about academic lessons; it's about life lessons that shape their entire being, including their spiritual health.

During my time in foster care, I narrowly associated "education" with formal schooling—elementary through college. No one introduced me to the broader concept of education that included valuable life skills and personal development. Consequently, whenever someone tried to impart wisdom, I resisted, perceiving it as an attempt to control or change me, which I equated with erasing my history and identity.

*

However, education is undeniably the key to success and overcoming trauma. To engage Dreamers effectively, especially those skeptical about traditional forms of learning due to past traumas, we must broaden their understanding of education to include wellness education. This type of education aims to enhance their ambition, happiness, motivation, and overall health—socially, emotionally, mentally, physically, and spiritually.

Social-Emotional Education is crucial because it equips Dreamers with the skills necessary for life success. This includes the ability to manage emotions, build positive relationships, communicate effectively, and make responsible decisions. Dreamers with robust social-emotional skills can better handle stress, navigate adversity, and engage productively in the workplace. Furthermore, it fosters self-awareness and self-efficacy, empowering Dreamers to take initiative and be resilient.

*

CHAPTER 8: (E)DUCATION — "ELEVATE THEIR MINDSET"

Here are activities for daily practice:

1. Mindfulness Exercises: Encourage Dreamers to spend a few minutes each day on mindfulness to enhance self-awareness and emotional regulation.

2. Gratitude Journaling: Help them cultivate a positive mindset by writing down things they are grateful for each day.

3. Active Listening: Teach them to fully engage in conversations to foster empathy and strengthen relationships.

4. Collaborative Problem-Solving: Promote teamwork through group activities that require cooperative solutions.

Mental Health Education during significant life transitions are imperative. As Dreamers navigate new responsibilities and self-discovery, their mental health can significantly impact their overall well-being. Although, to engage Dreamers in mental health practices, it must be approached in a creative and inviting manner, not the normal therapy way.

*

Effective mental health practices include:

1. Stress Management Techniques: Such as yoga, meditation, or physical activities to reduce anxiety and stress.

2. Positive Self-Talk: Encourage Dreamers to challenge negative thoughts and reinforce their self-esteem with positive affirmations.

3. Arts Therapy: Engage Dreamers in creative outlets such as drawing, painting, music, or writing to help express emotions, process trauma, and promote mental well-being.

4. Mindfulness Practices: Teach Dreamers to focus on the present moment through breathing exercises, guided imagery, or journaling, fostering emotional regulation and reducing feelings of overwhelm.

5. Gratitude Exercises: Introduce daily practices like gratitude journaling to help Dreamers shift their focus toward positive aspects of their lives, enhancing emotional resilience.

CHAPTER 8: (E)DUCATION — "ELEVATE THEIR MINDSET"

Physical Health underpins a Dreamer's ability to tackle daily challenges and recover from setbacks. Activities that boost physical health, such as regular exercise, not only improve endurance but also enhance mental health by releasing endorphins, natural mood lifters.

Maintaining good physical health is crucial; it includes not only regular physical activity but also attending annual medical and dental check-ups to prevent health issues and ensure overall well-being. A balanced diet and sufficient sleep are essential for sustaining physical health, as they help regulate mood and improve resilience.

Effective physical health practices include:

1. Regular Exercise: Engage in activities like walking, cycling, or team sports to maintain physical fitness and boost mental health.

2. Nutritional Awareness: Educate on balanced diets that fuel the body and mind adequately.

3. Routine Health Check-ups: Encourage annual visits to healthcare professionals to monitor and maintain health.

*

4. Sleep Hygiene: Promote consistent sleep patterns to enhance physical recovery and mental clarity.

Spiritual Health is an integral part of a Dreamer's overall well-being, providing a deep sense of meaning and purpose in life. It helps Dreamers connect to something greater than themselves, whether through organized religion, personal beliefs, or a broader sense of spirituality.

To foster spiritual health, consider these practices:

1. Meditation and Prayer: Encouraging regular meditation or prayer can help Dreamers find peace and clarity, enhancing their spiritual journey.

2. Community Involvement: Engaging with a community that shares similar spiritual values can provide support and a sense of belonging.

3. Reflective Practices: Promoting activities like journaling or nature walks can help Dreamers explore their spiritual beliefs and feelings.

*

By expanding the concept of education to encompass these elements of wellness, we provide Dreamers with a holistic approach that prepares them for the complexities of life, including navigating the foster. care system. This comprehensive educational strategy ensures that Dreamers not only survive but thrive, equipped with the knowledge and skills to navigate their journeys confidently and healthily.

Chapter 9: (A)ccountability
"Let them own their choices!"

Accountability is a pivotal element in building resilience, particularly for Dreamers who have experienced trauma. Resilience—the capacity to recover quickly from difficulties—is crucial for these individuals, as they often encounter numerous challenges that can significantly impact their mental health and overall well-being. When Dreamers are encouraged to own their choices, they develop a sense of control and agency over their lives, empowering them to take proactive steps to improve their circumstances.

Dreamers, especially those from the foster care system, often have complex life experiences that can impair their ability to regulate emotions, communicate effectively, form healthy relationships, and respond constructively to life's challenges. Without a foundation of personal accountability, Dreamers may find themselves falling into destructive patterns such as substance abuse, criminal behavior, or social isolation.

*

CHAPTER 9: (A)CCOUNTABILITY "LET THEM OWN THEIR CHOICES"

Understanding the Role of Accountability

When Dreamers are held accountable for their actions, they are more likely to develop a resilience mindset that empowers them to face and overcome obstacles. For instance, recognizing the detrimental impact of substance abuse and taking responsibility for changing such behavior can be the first step toward recovery and positive change.

However, accountability is often missing from the lives of many Dreamers, particularly those in foster care. Negative behaviors might result in being moved from one home to another without discussing the choices that led to these actions. This approach can lead to a numbing effect towards accountability, where Dreamers feel they are just passed along without any real opportunity to learn from their actions or understand the importance of being accountable.

Facilitating Accountability

Accountability transforms Dreamers' lives by enabling them to develop positive relationships, take ownership of their actions, and build empowerment. Here's why it's crucial:

CHAPTER 9: (A)CCOUNTABILITY   "LET THEM OWN THEIR CHOICES"

1. **Positive Relationships:** Being accountable makes Dreamers more trustworthy and reliable, which can strengthen social connections and support networks. These relationships provide a source of emotional support and help build resilience.

2. **Empowerment through Ownership:** Accountability encourages Dreamers to take charge of their decisions, fostering a sense of empowerment.

3. **Resilience Building:** By taking responsibility, Dreamers develop healthy coping skills essential for managing life's stressors effectively.

4. **Support Networks:** A robust network of individuals who hold Dreamers accountable can offer guidance, emotional support, and encouragement, reinforcing a sense of community and belonging.

Effective Practices for Promoting Accountability

1. **Therapy and Support Groups:** These provide safe, non-judgmental spaces for Dreamers to explore their experiences

and learn to take responsibility for their actions.

2. **Educational Workshops:** Workshops on accountability can show its impact on personal and professional life, teaching Dreamers how their actions affect themselves and others.

3. **Mentorship Programs:** Connecting Dreamers with mentors who exemplify accountability and provide ongoing support and guidance.

Engagement Opportunities to Enhance Accountability

To help Dreamers understand and value accountability, engage them in the following activities:

1. **Personal Ownership Exercises:** Teach Dreamers to identify the strengths and challenges in their success plans, encouraging them to acknowledge their shortcomings and the reality of their situations.

2. **Proactive Problem Solving:** Cultivate an attitude focused on solutions rather than problems. Encourage Dreamers to ask themselves, "What else can I do?" to maintain momentum

toward their goals.

3. **Action-Oriented Tasks:** Highlight the importance of taking decisive actions to achieve tangible results. Show that accountability is not merely about acknowledging faults but actively working towards improvement.

4. **Organizational Skills Training:** Provide tools for better life management, such as using professional emails, maintaining a calendar, and setting SMART goals to transform ambitions into reality.

5. **Reflective Practices:** Daily self-reflection can help Dreamers develop self-awareness and pinpoint areas for personal growth. Techniques might include journaling, guided reflections, or mindfulness exercises.

Building Comprehensive Accountability

Expanding on these foundational practices, it is essential to integrate accountability into all aspects of a Dreamer's life. This integration should foster environments where Dreamers are encouraged to

CHAPTER 9: (A)CCOUNTABILITY — "LET THEM OWN THEIR CHOICES"

engage with community resources, participate in civic duties, and contribute positively to their environments. By weaving accountability into the fabric of their daily lives, Dreamers learn the value of their contributions to society and the importance of living up to their responsibilities and commitments.

Incorporating accountability into the educational curriculum can also play a significant role in reinforcing its importance. Schools and learning programs should aim to imbue students with a sense of responsibility not only for their academic tasks but also for their behavior towards peers and engagement within their broader community.

In summary, a well-rounded approach to fostering accountability can profoundly impact Dreamers, setting them on a path toward resilience, empowerment, and successful integration into society. This chapter emphasizes the necessity of accountability in personal development, particularly for Dreamers overcoming trauma, and highlights strategies to embed accountability in everyday practices and interactions.

*

Chapter 10: (M)otivation
"Define their WHY!"

Motivation is a vital skill that we must cultivate in our Dreamers. It provides them with the clarity to recognize their purpose and use it as a powerful force to overcome the challenges of life. To transform their dreams into realities, Dreamers must be motivated to set and actively pursue their goals. Without this driving force, they may lack direction, leading to poor daily decision-making and numerous setbacks. Yet, when motivation is clearly defined, these obstacles no longer serve as roadblocks but become stepping-stones to perseverance and resilience.

Understanding the Essence of Motivation:

- Dreamers should explore the multifaceted nature of motivation, learning how it varies from one individual to another.
- They should be encouraged to discover motivational tools and resources that resonate with their personal journey, integrating these into their daily routines to sustain their drive.

*

CHAPTER 10: (M)OTIVATION — "DEFINE THEIR WHY"

Identifying Personal Motivation:

A deep dive into self-discovery is essential for Dreamers to pinpoint what truly drives them. This process empowers them to articulate clearly what motivates them, turning abstract dreams into concrete goals.

The Power of Hope: Consider what wakes people up each morning, ready to tackle the day. For many, they hope their efforts will lead to tangible rewards—a fulfilling job, a comfortable home, a dependable car, or a loving family. Dreamers often seek familial approval, social status at school, or the exciting prospect of driving to school.

However, for Dreamers, particularly those from the foster care system, hope can be scarce. Neglect from families and the system's constraints, combined with the harsh labels imposed upon them, can make them feel left behind or less than their peers. This lack of hope often forces them to operate in survival mode, constantly searching for validation in moments, relationships, or communities.

Cultivating Self-Motivation: Equipping Dreamers with the tools for self-motivation allows them to navigate life independently, reducing their reliance on others and enhancing their ability to make decisions that align with their aspirations. Self-motivation not only drives them to achieve their goals but also instills a sense of accomplishment and self-worth.

Interactive Motivational Challenges:

1. **Motivational Media Exploration:**

Encourage Dreamers to watch at least 10 motivational videos, reflecting on the messages and how they apply to their lives.

Ask them to identify and document the themes that resonate most and why these messages inspire them.

2. **Expression Challenge:**

Challenge Dreamers to share their thoughts on their favorite motivational piece in a concise, 60-second explanation, focusing on why it impacts them.

This exercise helps Dreamer's practice articulating their thoughts and feelings clearly and confidently.

3. **Goal-Setting Workshops:**

Conduct workshops that guide Dreamers through the process of setting specific, measurable, achievable, relevant, and time-bound

CHAPTER 10: (M)OTIVATION — "DEFINE THEIR WHY"

(SMART) goals.

These sessions should encourage Dreamers to align their motivations with their long-term objectives, breaking down larger aspirations into manageable steps.

4. **Daily Motivation Logs:**

Introduce a daily practice of recording motivational thoughts, feelings, or quotes. This log can serve as a personal motivational resource that Dreamers can refer to whenever they need a boost.

This habit fosters a routine of reflection and self-encouragement, which is crucial for maintaining motivation.

5. **Community Motivation Sharing:**

Create a community board—either virtual or physical—where Dreamers can post motivational quotes, stories, or personal victories.

This shared space not only promotes a sense of community and support but also inspires others to pursue their goals with renewed vigor.

CHAPTER 10: (M)OTIVATION — "DEFINE THEIR WHY"

By embedding motivation deeply into the fabric of their development, we empower Dreamers to pursue their dreams with passion and resilience. This chapter is designed to inspire both mentors and Dreamers to cultivate a robust motivational framework that transforms potential setbacks into opportunities for growth and success.

Chapter 11: (S)pirituality
"Define their life purpose!"

Spirituality encompasses recognizing a feeling, belief, or understanding that there is something greater than oneself—something beyond mere human sensory experiences. It suggests that we are part of a divine whole, contributing to a purposeful unfolding of life in the universe. Engaging with spirituality is not just about seeking existential answers but also about enhancing one's physical and mental health. On a deeper level, spirituality fosters compassion, strengthens relationships, and boosts self-esteem.

For Dreamers from the foster care system, the journey toward identifying their life purpose and establishing a deep connection with spirituality presents a unique advantage. Often, individuals from more stable backgrounds rush through life's significant events, driven by the immediate needs of survival and daily responsibilities. They rarely have a moment to pause and reflect deeply on life's greater questions or to contemplate their experiences and challenges due to the constant pressure to move on to the next task.

*

However, Dreamers in the foster care system frequently find themselves in survival mode, too, facing the relentless urgency of personal and family crises without a stable support system. This can hinder their ability to pause and engage in reflection, as they must focus intently on navigating the complexities of their immediate environment. The lack of stability often forces Dreamers to continuously adapt, leaving little room for the kind of reflective pause that fosters deep spiritual connections.

Engaging with Spirituality:

1. **Understanding Spirituality:**
    - Encourage Dreamers to explore various spiritual concepts and belief systems to broaden their understanding.
    - Challenge them to articulate their spiritual beliefs and how these perspectives shape their view of the world.

2. **Cultivating Spiritual Relationships:**
    - Guide Dreamers in discovering how personal spirituality can be developed and reinforced in

- everyday life.
- Establish structured routines that integrate spiritual practices into their daily lives, enhancing their connection to their core beliefs.

3. **Routine for Service:**

    - Teach the importance of service and its profound impact on both personal growth and community well-being.
    - Help Dreamers identify areas where they feel drawn to contribute, understanding the personal and communal significance of their actions.

4. **Understanding Spiritual History:**

    - Encourage Dreamers to delve into the origins of the world or explore their beliefs about the beginnings of life.
    - Assist them in developing a personal understanding of life's meaning and the existence of everything around them.

CHAPTER 11: (S)PIRITUALITY   "DEFINE THEIR LIFE PURPOSE

Interactive Challenges for Spiritual Growth:

- **Spiritual Exploration Sessions:** Organize workshops or discussion groups where Dreamers can share and learn about different spiritual traditions and practices. This could involve guest speakers from various faith backgrounds or visits to different places of worship.

- **Daily Reflection Practice:** Introduce a daily journaling or meditation practice that encourages Dreamers to reflect on their spiritual experiences and the insights they gain. This can help solidify their understanding and appreciation of their spiritual journey.

- **Community Service Projects:** Facilitate opportunities for Dreamers to engage in community service. This helps them put their spiritual beliefs into action and see the tangible impact of their contributions to the community.

- **Spiritual Storytelling:** Create a platform for Dreamers to share their spiritual journeys and histories. This could be through digital storytelling, blog posts, or community presentations, allowing them to articulate their spiritual growth and how it influences their life choices.

By integrating spirituality into their development, Dreamers can transform their view of life from one of survival to one of meaningful engagement and purpose. This chapter aims to inspire both mentors and Dreamers to cultivate a robust framework of spirituality that not only defines their purpose but also transforms their potential setbacks into opportunities for profound personal growth and fulfillment.

Entrepreneur

Conclusion

SMART DREAMS is not just a program model but a transformational journey that equips young people with the tools to navigate their lives successfully. It is about making intentional choices that lead to a healthy, confident, and self-sufficient lifestyle. Through the strategies outlined in this book, we aim to leave a lasting impact, encouraging you to transform the lives of those you guide and mentor. The SMART DREAMS approach is not merely about setting goals; it's about creating a legacy of empowerment, one that continues well beyond our direct interactions with Dreamers. Every choice made, every challenge overcome, and every relationship nurtured is part of something bigger—a ripple effect that can inspire future generations.

As mentioned earlier, SMART DREAMS is a lifestyle rooted in intentional living. It aims to foster self-confidence, quality life, and resilience in Dreamers who, like many from the foster care system, often struggle with self-sufficiency and financial independence due to emotional barriers and past traumas. These hurdles can make it difficult to fully engage with opportunities, leading to short-term fixes rather than long-term fulfillment. But when Dreamers understand the power of intentional choices and their "WHY," they can begin to see beyond their current circumstances and realize their potential.

The SMART DREAMS journey doesn't end here. It begins now, with every Dreamer, every mentor, every SAFE team member reading this book and committing to the process. The transformation we seek for our Dreamers is possible, and it begins with fostering environments of trust, accountability, and unconditional support. The path forward is clear: when you empower a Dreamer with tools for self-confidence, self-sufficiency, and financial security, you are not just changing their life—you are changing the world they influence.

Let this be the moment you take everything you've learned and put it into action. Create spaces of connection, inspire change, and build a lasting legacy that will endure well beyond your direct involvement.

Today, 13 years later, I have used the SMART DREAMS lifestyle to transform my life, achieving not just self-confidence but also self-sufficiency and financial security.

Instead of becoming a statistic, I've turned my story into a platform of hope and inspiration for others. I've advocated for systemic change and created solutions for those raised in foster care, just like I was.

My journey has included helping to shape several of Florida's laws to improve the foster care system and playing a pivotal role in the design and development of statewide programs. One of these is **My JumpVault**, a software platform providing instant access to vital health and personal records for youth, foster parents, and social workers. This tool ensures better communication and accessibility within the foster care system (for more information, visit www.myjumpvault.org).

In 2015, I launched **My Jumpstart**, a youth development organization offering experiential learning services designed to foster confidence, strategy, and resilience in young adults transitioning to independence. My Jumpstart is widely recognized for hosting the **My Jumpstart to Independence Conferences**, empowering young people across the state of Florida.

Building on this foundation, in 2020, I founded **Dreams And Success Homes, Inc. (DASH)** and **DASH Foundation, Inc.**, a social impact initiative that combines therapeutic empowerment coaching with a statewide housing network. DASH now stands as one of Florida's fastest growing housing providers for foster care and homeless young adults, offering 58 beds across five counties. These therapeutic empowerment coaching homes support young adults in building personal confidence, achieving self-sufficiency, and gaining financial security.

As the President and CEO of DASH, I have raised over $1.5 million to establish this impactful statewide housing network. Looking forward, DASH plans to expand its reach significantly, launching 50 additional homes to serve a total of 300 young adults annually.

My leadership journey and commitment to creating lasting change have been recognized with several prestigious honors. These include being named in **Forbes NEXT 1000** for bold and inspiring entrepreneurs, **40 Under 40: Black Leaders of Today & Tomorrow** by Legacy Magazine, **National REFCA**

Champion by Treehouse Foundation, and receiving the **Soaring Eagle Award** from my alma mater, Tallahassee Community College.

Through SMART DREAMS, I am redefining what it means to pursue your dreams and become a success story as an alumnus who aged out of a failed human service system. My journey stands as a testament to the power of resilience, the strength of intentional living, and the potential for impactful change when we empower others to thrive.

And now, with the guidance of this book, you can also break barriers and rewrite narratives, ensuring that every Dreamer is equipped with the tools, support, and confidence to turn their dreams into reality. You will build a future where every Dreamer you serve not only survives but thrives—boldly and confidently embracing their potential and transforming their dreams into achievements.

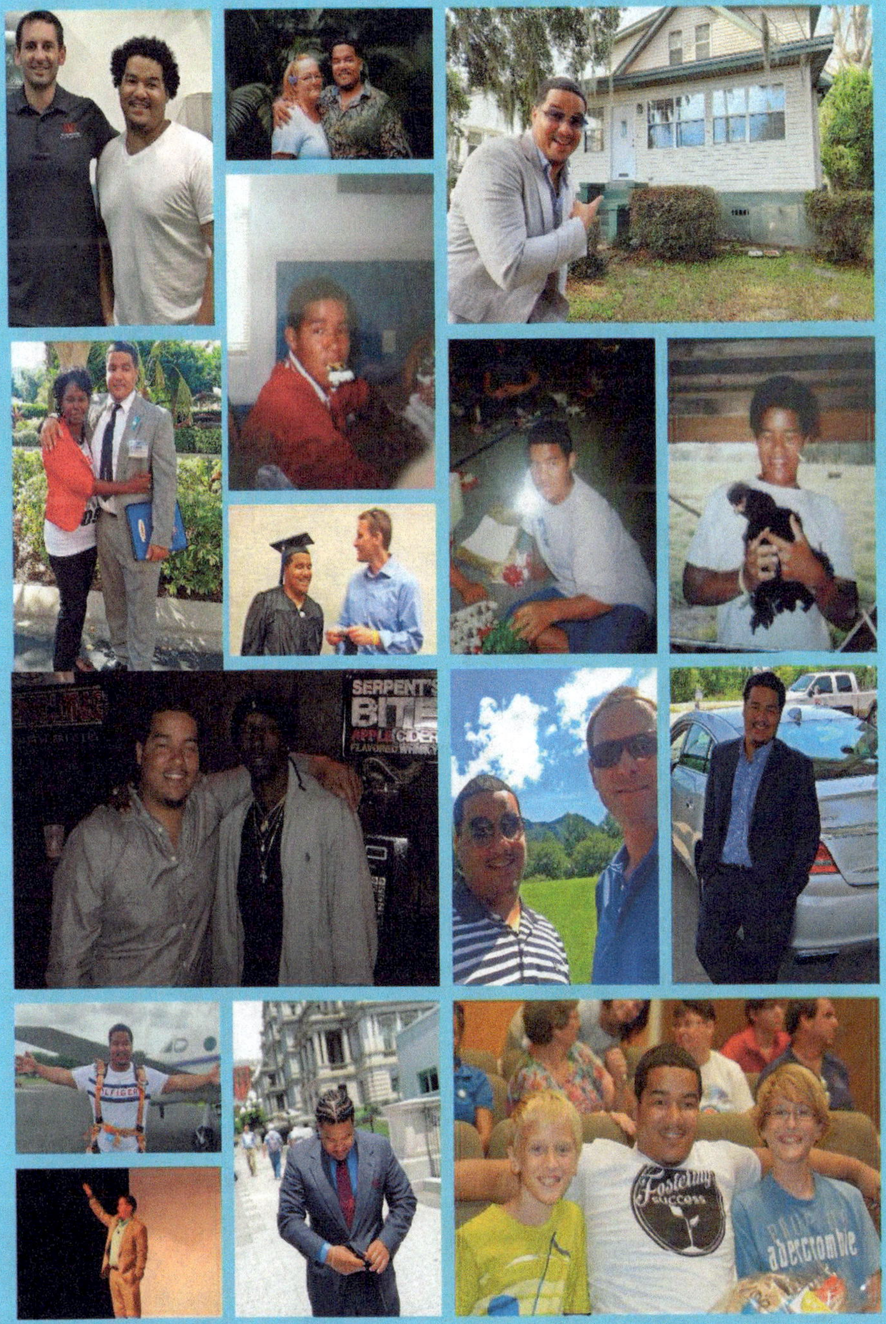
SERPENT'S
BITE
APPLE CIDER
abercrombie

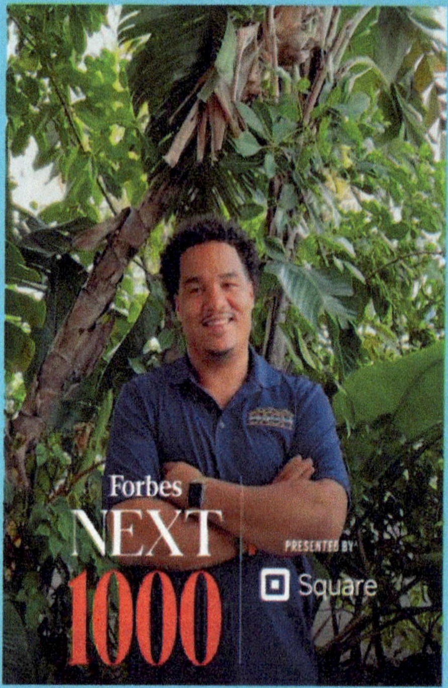
Forbes
NEXT
1000
PRESENTED BY
Square

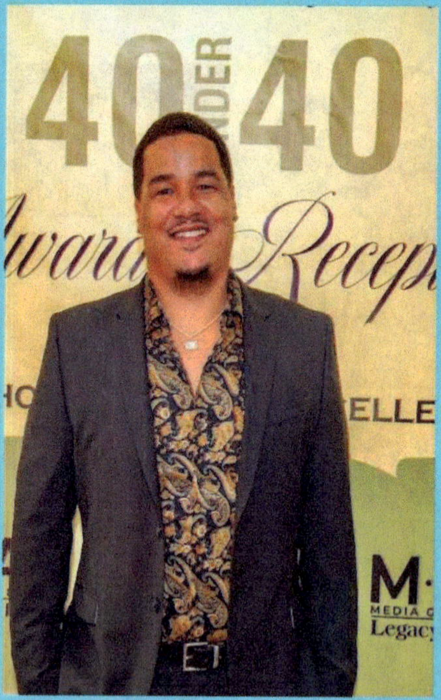
40
40

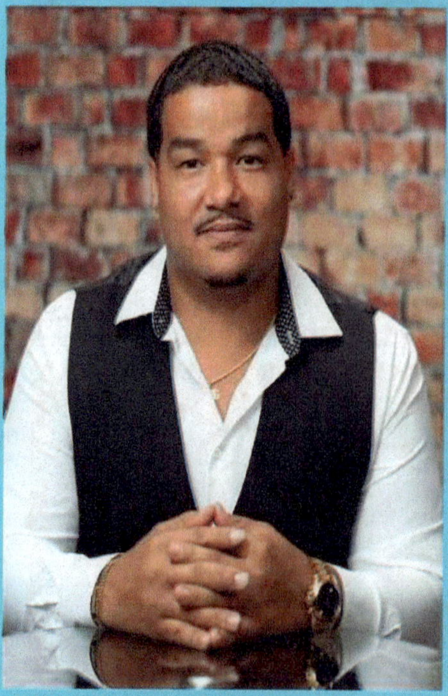

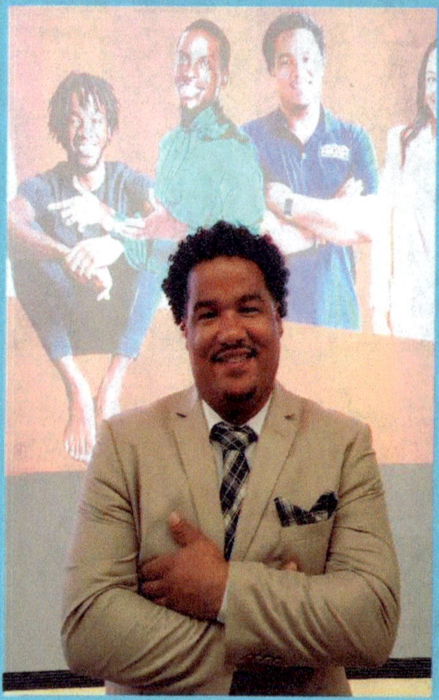

Afterword: SMART DREAMS Coaching

As you've journeyed through this book, you've gained insights into connecting deeply with your Dreamers and cultivating in them a mindset ready to conquer life's challenges. Now, it's about applying those lessons to help your Dreamers manage their struggles, heal from past traumas, and break free from cycles that have held them back. Coaches may be foster parents, professional staff, or any adult who is completely invested in advocating for the Dreamer's well-being and prioritizing their growth and development.

Phased Approach to Empowerment

The journey from dependence to independence for Dreamers follows a phased approach. Each phase is structured to help Dreamers gradually build the skills and confidence they need to achieve a life of autonomy and success. As a coach, your role is to introduce the following phases to your Dreamers to structure their SMART DREAMS development. You will notice that each phase encourages Dreamers to increase the amount of time they devote to education/employment/entrepreneurship which ensures they are gradually building to optimal success.

*

As a coach, you play a key role in communicating with your Dreamers to jointly assess their readiness to advance to each phase.

Phase 1: SMART DREAMS (Self-Confidence)

Weekly Hours for Dreamers to Invest:

- 20+ hours: Education/Employment/Entrepreneurship
- 5+ hours: Personal Development
- 5 hours: Service

Expected Outcomes/Skills:

- Mastery of SMART Goal Setting
- Development of Personal Values
- Enhancement of Social-Emotional Skills

Phase 2: DASH 2 Independence (Self-Sufficiency)

Weekly Hours for Dreamers to Invest:

- 30+ hours: Education, Employment, Entrepreneurship
- 5+ hours: Personal Development
- 5 hours: Service

Expected Outcomes/Skills:

- Acquisition of Essential Life Skills
- Attainment of Career Education/Training to achieve independence without government assistance

Phase 3: DASH 2 Freedom (Financial Security)

Weekly Hours for Dreamers to Invest:

- 40+ hours: Education/Employment/Entrepreneurship
- 5+ hours: Personal Development
- 5 hours: Service

Expected Outcomes/Skills:

- Build wealth through two options:
    - Homeownership purchasing your 1st home.
    - Entrepreneurship establishing a business that produces at least $600+ a month in profit.

Structured Routine for Success

Establishing a structured routine is critical for your Dreamer's growth. It provides the framework for empowerment, allowing Dreamers to live confidently and pursue their goals effectively. This structured routine includes two essential meetings with you as a coach:

1. **SMART DREAMS 1:1 Meeting:**
   - A personalized, therapeutic empowerment session focusing on the DASH Life Productivity Assessment (available through SMART DREAMS software offered by DASH Foundation, Inc.), SMART Goal Setting, and DREAMS Mindset Assessment.
   - In this meeting, you will review the Dreamer's activities from the previous week, assess their progress, and set new goals that are Specific, Measurable, Attainable, Realistic, and Time-bound.

2. **SMART DREAMS Dinner Group Meeting:**
   - This weekly group meeting combines meal preparation

- with therapeutic discussions, creating an environment of belonging and community.

- During the meal, you'll discuss SMART DREAMS topics, challenges, and the progress made over the week, encouraging Dreamers to share their experiences and learn from one another.

Engage and Inspire

To effectively implement the SMART DREAMS model, it's important to incorporate interactive and engaging activities that align with each phase:

- **Productivity Workshops:** Help Dreamers develop time management and organization skills so they can meet the demands of the DASH Life phases.

- **Goal Visualization Sessions:** Inspire Dreamers to visualize their long-term goals through creative exercises like vision boards or storytelling, reinforcing the importance of their SMART goals.

- **Community Engagement Projects:** Involve Dreamers in meaningful community service, helping them see the impact of their actions while developing leadership and service-oriented mindsets.

Empowering the Future

As you embark on implementing the SMART DREAMS framework, remember that this journey is not just about guiding Dreamers through phases—it's about transforming lives. Each interaction, each goal achieved, and each moment of growth has the potential to create ripples that extend far beyond the present.

You hold in your hands the tools to help Dreamers turn their obstacles into opportunities, their traumas into triumphs, and their dreams into realities. By creating environments of trust, structure, and accountability, you empower young people to live confidently, equipped with the skills and mindset to thrive. Your role is pivotal in helping them break free from the chains of their past and step boldly into their future.

*

Let the principles in this book be a living blueprint for lasting change, not only in the lives of the Dreamers you serve but also in the communities they will go on to impact. Through SMART DREAMS, we can build a legacy of empowerment, where every young person knows that their dreams aren't just possibilities—they are inevitable.

Interactive Vision Board Experience

Instructions: These next pages are for YOU, the reader, to DREAM BIG. Use these vision board pages to draw, write, or glue in pictures that represent your future. Let your imagination lead the way!

My Future Starts Here

Draw a picture of YOU in the future. What do you look like? What are you doing? What's around you?

What makes you feel powerful about your future?

My SAFE Team (Relationships)

List or draw the people who make you feel safe, supported, and loved.

- Who will you call when you need help?

- Who helps you stay strong?

My SAFE Team includes:

1.

2.

3.

My Dream Career

What job do you want when you grow up? Draw or write about what your workspace might look like.

My dream career is: _____

Why do I want this job? _____

My Career Tools

Every great career needs tools! List or draw what skills or items you'll need for your job.

I need to learn or have:

1.

2.

3.

My Dream Home (Lifestyle)

Draw your dream home. Where is it? What's inside?

My home will feel like: _____

I will live in: _____

My Room Inside My Dream Home

Design your dream room. What color is it? What makes it comfortable and fun?

Things I want in my room:

-

-

*

Entertainment & Self-Care (Bucket List)

What are some fun things you want to do just for YOU? Make a bucket list!

My self-care & fun goals:

• Go to _____

• Try _____

• Learn _____

A Day of Fun

Draw your perfect self-care day from morning to night. What are you doing to take care of YOU?

My favorite way to relax is: _____

My Wealth Vision (Money Goals)

How much money do you want to save or earn? What will you do with it?

I want to save: $_____

I want to invest in: _____

My Budget Map

Create a simple budget. Draw or list where your money goes.

Where my money goes:

• Save:

• Spend:

• Share:

My Future Life Timeline

Draw or write a timeline of the goals you want to achieve over the next 5-10 years.

In 1 year I will: _____

In 5 years I will: _____

In 10 years I will: _____

My SMART DREAMS Commitment Page

Sign your name and write down one thing you will start doing TODAY to build your future.

I commit to becoming my best self by: _____

Signed: _____

Date: _____

> *"Your DREAMS are not just aspirations; they are the blueprint for the life you're destined to create."*

"The power to transform your life begins with the courage to define your own SMART path."

> *"Be specific with your dreams, stay motivated with your actions, and let your goals shape your destiny."*

"Every step you take is an investment in the resilient, empowered version of yourself."

> *"True strength comes from within — focus on your mind, body, and spirit to build the future you deserve."*

> *"Timing is everything — trust the process and approach each moment with purpose."*

"You are the driver of your own life — take control, steer confidently, and create the journey you desire."

"The relationships you build today shape the foundation for the life you want tomorrow."

> *"Education is the key to unlocking the doors of opportunity — embrace it, expand it, live it."*

"Accountability is the bridge between intentions and achievements. Surround yourself with those who support your growth."

"Your 'why' fuels your motivation — stay rooted in it and watch your resilience soar."

_____

_____

_____

_____

_____

_____

_____

_____

_____

_____

> *"Spirituality is your compass, guiding you to a life filled with purpose, meaning, and limitless potential."*

From the depths of my heart—thank you.

Thank you for taking this journey through SMART DREAMS. Whether you are a Dreamer yourself, a mentor, a caregiver, a professional, or a champion of change, your decision to read this book means you're part of a powerful movement: one that transforms trauma into purpose, pain into progress, and doubt into dreams fulfilled.

This book was born from my lived experience, but it was written for you—to inspire, empower, and equip you with the mindset and tools to guide Dreamers toward a life of self-confidence, resilience, and freedom. And most importantly, to believe in your WHY again and keep your commitment to service. You now carry the spark of SMART DREAMS. My challenge to you? Light the path for someone else. Show up. Speak life. Coach with compassion. Be the SAFE team someone never had.

If this book moved you, helped you, or simply reminded you that purpose still lives within the pain—you're not alone. I'd love to stay connected with you and hear how SMART DREAMS is showing up in your world.

Visit me at: www.SMARTDREAMSCeo.com

Follow and connect on social media:

@SMARTDREAMSCEO

Let's keep this movement alive. Together, we can ensure that every Dreamer doesn't just survive—but thrives, with boldness, healing, and purpose

Made in the USA
Columbia, SC
09 May 2025